"*Root Beer Lady* is wonderfully written and easy to read, loaded with facts and interesting stories about a captivating, one-of-a-kind lady and the unique area of our country that she called home."

Linda Fryer, Administrative Director
Ely Chamber of Commerce

"Great reading . . . Dorothy Molter epitomizes what the Boundary Waters is all about. Future generations need to recognize the importance of her contribution to this area."

Woods Davis
Tom and Woods' Moose Lake Wilderness Canoe Trips

"Bob caught Dorothy's spirit. Reading this book is like a stroll through Dorothy's life."

Bea Brophey
Dorothy Molter Foundation

"Dorothy's passing left a legacy of history that will always be an important part of the Boundary Waters Canoe Area Wilderness. She will always hold a special place in the heart of many U.S. Forest Service employees."

Roger Baker
District Ranger of U.S. Forest Service
Kawishiwi Ranger District 1986-1990

"Dorothy is a true legend, one of the finest people I ever met. Boy Scouts and Girl Scouts from around the world enjoyed stopping at the Isle of Pines for a cold root beer."

Sandy Bridges
Northern Tier National High Adventure
Boy Scouts of America

written and illustrated by
Bob Cary

Pfeifer-Hamilton

Pfeifer-Hamilton Publishers
210 West Michigan
Duluth MN 55802-1908 218-727-0500

Root Beer Lady: The Story of Dorothy Molter

Printed in the United States of America by Versa Press Inc.
10 9 8 7 6 5 4

Publisher: Donald A Tubesing
Editorial Director: Susan Gustafson
Assistant Editor: Patrick Gross
Art Director: Joy Morgan Dey

Library of Congress Cataloging in Publication Data
92-61331

ISBN 0-938586-68-8

Dedication

It is customary to dedicate a book to someone;
but to tell the truth, it is the dedication of my wife, Lil,
to our life together that has made it all possible—
besides paddling the front end of the canoe
all over much of North America, carrying her share
of the packsacks over countless portages for more than
four decades, and finding time to raise a
couple of daughters along the way.

C O N T E N T S

Acknowledgments

A number of people contributed to the writing of this book, people who furnished information, photos, and anecdotes concerning Dorothy Molter. I cannot list them all, but some of the important sources were Alice Swenson, Dorothy's niece, who spent many summers on Knife Lake and who graciously shared numerous photos and much information concerning Dorothy's life; Steve Molter, Dorothy's nephew, who has been a source of information over many years; Bea Brophey and members of the Dorothy Molter Memorial Foundation; Larry and Myrt Sernak; Gladys and Laurel Bennett; Bernie and Joyce Carlson; John and Peg Rosett; Dick Abrahamson; "Knife Lake Pete" Cosme; bush pilot Chick Beel; Quetico Park naturalist Shirley Peruniak; publisher of the *Ely Echo*, Anne Wognum; publisher of the *Ely Miner*, Columbia Childers; Louise Thureen; Emery Bulinski; and all those who may be considered friends of Dorothy and Dorothy's Angels.

Special help came from Jim Hinds and Jerry Jussila of the U.S. Forest Service, who provided much of the information on Dorothy's later years on Knife Lake.

Foreword

From 1930 to 1986, a period of fifty-six years, the Isle of Pines at Knife Lake, along the Minnesota–Ontario border, provided the setting for a drama that the wilderness had never seen before and will never see again. The star was Dorothy Molter, a young Chicago nurse who opted for a life on the northern frontier, thirty miles from Ely, the nearest city. This book tells of that life as fully as I could assemble the facts. May you enjoy reading this story as much as I enjoyed gathering this information and knowing this kind, gracious, talented, and very courageous lady.

ISLE OF PINES

BOUNDARY WATERS
CANOE AREA WILDERNESS

ELY

DULUTH

MINNESOTA

Fall Lake

Fernberg Road

Winton

Garden Lake

Kawishiwi River

Ely

Dorothy Molter
Memorial

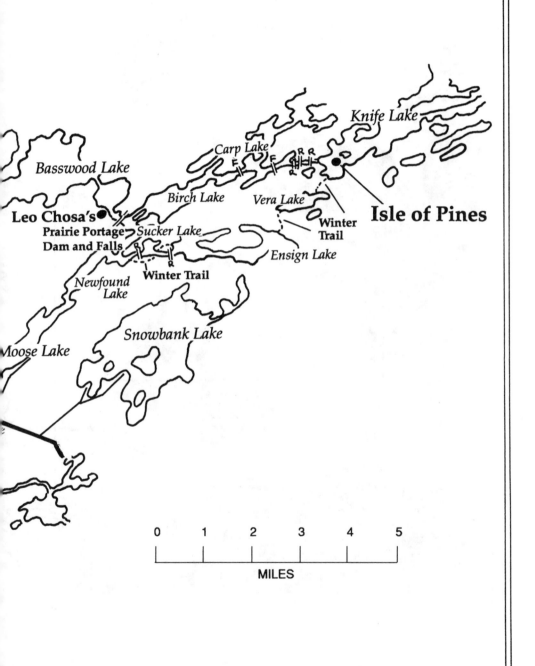

Knife Lake

Carp Lake

F F

R R
H H
R

Basswood Lake

Birch Lake

Vera Lake

Isle of Pines

Leo Chosa's

Prairie Portage

Dam and Falls

Sucker Lake

R

**Winter
Trail**

Winter Trail

Ensign Lake

Newfound
Lake

Moose Lake

Snowbank Lake

```
0     1     2     3     4     5

MILES
```

The Discovery

THE INSTANT the canoe bow touched the sandy beach below the rapids, Dorothy vaulted over the gunwale and sprinted up the time-worn portage leading to Knife Lake.

"It wasn't that I wouldn't help carry my share," she recalled later, "but every portage was a brand new experience and I just had to run and see what was on the other side."

The view took her breath away. Knife Lake stretched clear blue and shimmering between granite-ribbed, wooded shores. To her right, a torrent of clear water poured out of the lake, churning in creamy froth through a scarred wooden sluiceway, a remnant of the logging era some two decades earlier. Through that sluice had gone several million board feet of white and Norway pine logs, pushed, pried, and floated downstream to Basswood Lake and from there to Fall Lake and the roaring, screeching lumber mills at Winton.

Overhead, a squadron of white herring gulls shrilled a greeting as they circled effortlessly on translucent black-tipped wings. Even the presence of pesky blackflies, which Dorothy swatted with dedication, couldn't mar the scene for the city-raised twenty-three year old. Exhilarated, she turned on her heel and dashed back down the rocky trail to the spot where her impatient father sorted out duffle and groceries to carry across.

Used to issuing orders, "Cap" Molter had divided the loads between himself, his wife, his brother, his daughter Dorothy, and the fifth member of the group, Cap's railroad coworker, on the trip's five portages. One square-stern canoe-and-motor, towing a big paddle canoe, had carried people and duffle on the fourteen-mile ride through Newfound, Sucker, Birch, Carp, Melon, and Seed lakes from the access on Moose Lake.

More than just an enthusiastic angler, Cap was incurably addicted to sport fishing. The lure of trophy northern pike and walleyes had drawn him to big Basswood Lake, near Ely, the previous year. While fishing on that broad body of angling water, he heard of a new resort recently opened on the Minnesota-Ontario border, far up in the back country—a resort that could be reached only by canoe or float plane. Informed that Knife Lake not only held whopper walleyes and northern pike but was famous for sleek, silvery lake trout up to forty pounds, Cap immediately corresponded with resort operator Bill Berglund to schedule a fishing expedition.

The original plans did not include Dorothy. "I was a substitute . . . a fill-in," she remembered later. Cap and his wife Myrtle (Dorothy's stepmother), Cap's brother, and two railroad pals made up the initial group. At the last minute, one of the men had to cancel, and Cap invited Dorothy to go along. Dorothy enjoyed fishing, although not with her father's single-minded intensity. On vacation before her final year of nursing school at Chicago's Auburn Park Hospital, she was looking for a summer job. But at the height of the Great Depression, jobs of any kind were scarce, so joining the fishing expedition posed no great financial sacrifice. And this trip offered an opportunity to see a piece of the North Country that she had previously only read about.

As the outboard had powered the two wood-and-canvas craft up the border lakes between the United States and Canada, endless discoveries greeted Dorothy. Their friendly guide showed her deer and bear tracks in the mud along Carp Portage. He aimed a forefinger at an eagle's nest on the north shore of Carp Lake and laughingly pointed out a pair of formally dressed black-and-white loons when she asked what was creating that "unearthly, mournful cry." He astounded her by dipping cupped hands into Seed Lake for a long, cool drink, noting that the water in these lakes was probably far more pure than the water coming out of the kitchen tap at her home in Chicago. Along the portage paths she noted low-growing mats of bunchberries with their shiny green leaves and brilliant, star-shaped white flowers. Wild roses just barely poked their pink heads out of the buds. On Melon Lake, a crested hen merganser and a thick-bodied black duck led separate lines of fluffy recently hatched young along the edges of newly emerged cattails.

Now, from Knife Portage it took only minutes for the two heavily laden craft to round the point into the sheltered bay where Berglund's headquarters cabin was located. As the guide shut off the outboard motor, the resort owner strode to the dock, hand extended in greeting. At six-foot-three, lean and hard from years on canoe, snowshoe, and sled dog trails as a guide, trapper, lumberjack, and game warden, he presented the calm, self-confident image of the storied North Country woodsman. Isle of Pines appeared exactly as his letters had described. Simple rustic log cabins stood back among the towering trees.

Owned originally by an official of the Swallow & Hopkins Lumber Company, the island's tall white and Norway pines had been spared the ax and saw. Berglund purchased Isle of Pines and two smaller adjacent islands, nine acres in all, on contract, intending to pay them off from the resort operation. In addition to the four cabins, the camp included a log boathouse on the beach and a small storage building, which had been a cabin salvaged from the logging company houseboat.

With a lot of handshaking, laughing, and good-natured banter, the party unloaded the canoes and made their way to their respective cabins. The men could scarcely take time to stow their duffle before rigging their fishing tackle and hurrying back to the dock, intent on doing battle with those fabled lake trout. Somewhat less stressed, Dorothy and her stepmother elected to stay in camp, arrange their belongings in order, and acclimate themselves a bit. As Dorothy reached up to place some clothing on the cabin shelf, a rustling and scratching of tiny claws preceded the appearance of a tiny striped chipmunk, which hit the cabin floor, bounded toward the sink, paused for a tail-shaking series of chirps, and then escaped through a hole in the log chinking.

Dorothy had barely recovered from this when a knock sounded at the screened cabin door. Berglund entered with an armload of split wood for the barrel stove. He laughed softly when Dorothy told him about her tiny wild visitor, strode to the tin bread box alongside the sink, lifted the lid, and retrieved a few crusts of bread. Motioning for Dorothy to follow, Berglund stepped outside and looked up into the trees. Holding a bit of bread lightly in his fingertips, he whistled softly. An answering call from the pines was followed by the soft swoosh of wings, as a gray Canada jay dropped down to Berglund's shoulder. The bird boldly cocked its head sidewise, plucked the crust from the man's fingers, and flew off into the trees.

"Here—try it yourself." Berglund handed a crust to Dorothy. She held up her hand tentatively and the jay curved down, landing on a nearby branch. The bird traded glances with her, determined there was no danger, swooped in, plucked the crust, and vanished.

"Are all the birds this tame?" Dorothy asked in wonder.

Berglund chuckled. "No, but the jays and chickadees are—and the squirrels and chipmunks will eat out of your hand." He

Bill Berglund

turned on his heel and retreated down the path, leaving Dorothy to ponder this bit of news. She quickly darted back inside, found one more leftover crust in the tin bread box, and went back out to find another bird. Seeing none, she sat on the warm wooden porch steps, looking up into the trees. Her hand with the crust dangled alongside her knee, and suddenly she felt a slight tug. Dorothy looked down just in time to see the chipmunk vanish with the piece of bread. "Why, you little dickens," she laughed. It was the first enactment of a scene that would be repeated endlessly in years to come.

With time to kill before dinner, Dorothy followed a shaded trail through the pines to the Point Cabin. She then circled along the island shore, stepping around clumps of low-growing juniper, and finally scrambled up on a smooth outcrop overlooking the lake. From this perch she could see straight across to the bay going into Portage Lake, watch the sunlight shimmering on the waves like blue sequins, and listen to the slup-slup of waves breaking into the shallows and washing around the shoreline boulders.

The forest across the bay stretched as far as she could see, a vast carpet of emerald birch and aspen leaves interspersed with spires of dark green fir and spruce. This was part of a huge wild area, part of the new Superior National Forest, so designated by President Theodore Roosevelt in 1909. On the adjacent Canadian side, the Quetico Forest and Game Reserve had been similarly created in 1909 and would later become the eighteen-hundred-square-mile Quetico Provincial Park. Now, in 1930, an international coalition of conservationists was engaged in a bitter fight in the courts and in the U.S. Congress to curb an attempt by wealthy power interests to place a series of eighty-foot-high electrical generating dams along the border, which would obliterate the existing lake system and permanently flood the heart of the wilderness.

As Dorothy sat atop the smooth outcrop, she couldn't know

that one day all that international pushing and shoving would directly affect her life. She only knew that this huge area was something wonderful and completely different from anything she had ever known. She breathed deeply the pure smoke-free air, noted the clean wave-washed rocks along the shore, and pondered the fact that people in this area actually obtained their drinking water at their very doorstep. Her attention was alerted by a movement on the shoreline. Quickly, furtively, a mink bounced from rock to rock, darting, pausing, turning its head left and right, then diving into the lake. In a moment it emerged with a crawfish, darted under some tree roots, and then vanished. While absorbing this bit of woodland theater, Dorothy heard a chattering cry from overhead and saw a small, pointed form shoot headfirst into the water, emerging instantly, then climbing on a blur of wingbeats to a dead limb, there to sit, dining on a minnow. Dorothy stared at the bird, recognizing the blue-and-white plumage, the sharp bill and upright crest of a kingfisher. Her attention riveted to the agile little bird, she didn't see the brown object moving over the surface of the lake until its V-wake cut almost into the shore. A wedge-shaped head with tiny black eyes stared unblinking over the three-foot section of freshly-cut alder branch locked firmly in a big set of yellowed incisors. Although she had never seen one before, Dorothy knew from books she had read and from visits to the Field Museum that this was a beaver—a real, live, wild beaver. Motionless, she stared at the mammal which stared back, trying to figure out what strange figure was on the rock ledge. Then Dorothy shifted her position to see better and the startled animal nosed over, slammed the water with its "tail-ker-whoomp!" and vanished. Dorothy jumped at the sound, which was "almost like a cannon going off," she recalled.

The chattering kingfisher flew off down the shore. The scene reverted to silence, broken only by the sighing wind in the overhead pine boughs. Dorothy ran a hand over her forehead and pushed back the thatch of dark brown hair. *This is incredible!*

she thought. *To sit in one place and see a kingfisher, a mink, and a beaver! What an amazing country.* And then her thoughts drifted back to distant Chicago, to days of growing up and attending school, to how hard she was working to get her registered nurse's license. Her plan since high school had been to support herself in Chicago through a life dedicated to the nursing profession.

She knew she wanted to be a nurse, but she was no longer sure about Chicago.

Moving North

Dorothy Louise Molter was born May 6, 1907, in Arnold, Pennsylvania, a small town just up the Allegheny River from Pittsburgh, as the third of Mattie and John "Cap" Molter's six children. Cap's job with the Baltimore and Ohio Railroad police took him out of town for days at a time, leaving Mattie with the main responsibility for rearing and disciplining the brood. Each youngster, as he or she came along, was expected to assume a share of the household chores, help the younger brothers and sisters, and excel in school.

Dorothy was a bright student in second grade when tragedy struck the family: Mattie died after a short illness, leaving John a widower with six youngsters. At this confusing and painful time, Cap tried to maintain family unity, but absences due to his work made it difficult. Various relatives attempted to board one or more members of the family, but this apparently caused more anguish. To keep his brood together, Cap placed them in a Cincinnati orphanage, where they had regular contact and mutual support and could visit with him when he was off-duty.

11

In 1919, Cap remarried. His new wife, Myrtle, helped bring the family together again in a new home in Garrett, Indiana. From there, they moved to Chicago, where they rented a large white frame home on Lagoon Avenue. The neighborhood of "Chicago style" bungalows circled a tree-lined lagoon that provided a gathering place for neighborhood kids, who caught sunfish in the summer and skated on the frozen surface in the winter.

Dorothy completed grade school, then enrolled in the brand new Calumet High School, an educational showplace with a new faculty, new programs, and high academic standards. Dorothy, who excelled in both classwork and sports, enjoyed school at Cal High. When developers bought the Molter home as the site of a new apartment complex and the family had to move, Dorothy continued at Cal High even though it meant a five-mile walk each day.

Dorothy, a strong, agile, and determined athlete, made her mark in basketball, volleyball, tennis, and swimming. An expert shot and a member of the school rifle team for four years, she won the girl's city championship in competition at the old Chicago Colosseum in 1925. At that time she had no way of knowing that her marksmanship would one day come in handy when she had to procure a winter's meat supply in the North Country wilderness or dispatch an unruly bear. Dorothy pursued her interest in writing by serving as a reporter for the school newspaper, the *Calnuz*, and as a staff member of the school yearbook in her junior and senior years. In the 1927 yearbook, under her photo, appears this description: "Athletic, quiet, and earnest."

Unfortunately, not many sources of employment existed in 1927 for athletic, quiet, and earnest young women who were dead shots. Dorothy turned her sights to a nursing career, enrolling for training at nearby Auburn Park Hospital. Just before her final year in nurse's training she first visited Knife Lake with Cap and Myrtle, the visit that would change her life.

MOVING NORTH

The fishing party's train ride to Ely seemed like a ride back into history. Lumberjacks, miners, prospectors, tradesmen, and vacationers crowded the Duluth Missabe and Iron Range Railroad cars. The train stopped at a dozen places to let off blueberry pickers from Duluth, who carried buckets, baskets, even wash boilers—it would pick them up again at every whistle stop and switch on the way back to Duluth at night.

Trains unloaded at the Ely Depot, where newcomers landed in the midst of a bustling city of over 6,000, a mix of iron miners, woods people, trappers, moonshiners, merchants, clerks, the righteous, and the not-so-righteous. Resorts springing up in and on the edge of the wilderness catered to the cream of America's sporting gentry—and a few of the dregs. The Forest Hotel on Sheridan Street provided a thriving clearinghouse for every type, coming and going, with Vertin's Cafe crammed to the walls on Saturday nights. The Ely Commercial Club had coined the phrase "Ely—Playground of the Nation," which was printed in the *Ely Miner* newspaper and displayed wherever Ely was advertised.

The mines formed the area's economic backbone. The first, the Chandler, had opened in 1888, the same year the city was incorporated. Then came the Pioneer and the Zenith, two of the more productive and more dangerous mines on the Vermilion Range. In 1930, the Pioneer and Zenith mines shipped iron to the world by the millions of tons. Some smaller lumber operations still functioned. The big mills like the St. Croix and Swallow & Hopkins at Winton were long gone, but Cyrille Fortier lumbered on Farm Lake and up the Kawishiwi Chain, floating logs down to his mill at Garden Lake. A number of notorious speakeasies dispensed beer and hard liquor surreptitiously to the thirsty in the Ely area, but fewer than a dozen churches served the residents' spiritual needs.

Dorothy stepped into this world in 1930, her eyes wide in amazement at a sprawling, brawling frontier community just beginning to assume a semblance of respectability.

MOVING NORTH

From Ely an hour's drive by gravel road brought travelers to Moose Lake, the jumping-off point for wilderness trips to the North and to Berglund's Resort to the east on Knife Lake. The resort at Isle of Pines gave somewhat of a shock to a young lady brought up in fairly upscale middle-class city surroundings. Owner Bill Berglund had correctly judged that a market existed for wilderness vacations, but he had scant funds to develop it. The layout comprised four spare log cabins, one dating back to the logging days. Adjacent to the resort dock, a big iron spike driven into the rock showed where rafts of white pine logs had been anchored in the bay prior to being run down the sluice at the west end of the lake. Those log drives passed through Melon, Seed, and Carp lakes, to Birch, and thence to Basswood Lake and the lumber mills at Winton.

A widower of fifty-six, Bill had migrated to the area following the logging companies. Born in New London, Minnesota, on August 4, 1874, he was one of three children of hardworking Finnish immigrant parents. Eventually he landed in Winton, where he worked as a lumberjack, trapper, and game warden before purchasing Isle of Pines and building it into a rough wilderness angler' camp. Knife Lake was one in the string of bluewater lakes and rivers that made up the historic French voyageurs' fur trade route stretching from Lake Superior to the Arctic. Berglund liked to point out diagonal ax scars on some of the big trees, marks left from the days of birchbark canoes, when paddlers notched pines for pitch to plug leaks in the seams. "Knife Lake," he noted, was the direct translation of *Mookamon Zaaga'igan*, the Ojibwa name for this lake, where native people for centuries had chipped tools and weapons from a particular ledge of rock.

Despite the difference in their ages, during the summer of 1930 Dorothy and Bill found they had a lot in common, particularly in regard to wilderness scenery, wildlife, and history. When Dorothy returned to Isle of Pines the next summer, she had finished her training as a professional nurse and arrived self-assured and confident of her ability. She impressed Bill with the speed with which she learned to swing an ax or handle a canoe paddle, to know the names and tracks of various animals, and to identify birds. And she surprised him with her strength as she flipped up eighty-pound packsacks with the ease of a veteran guide. He offered her a summer job, which she gratefully accepted, thrilled to be spending time in such incredibly beautiful country.

In 1931, the logger's axes and saws had been silent on Knife Lake for a decade. While the Canadian shore towered with virgin pines, new growth on the United States side consisted of aspen, birch, and balsam, from ten to fifteen feet tall, sprouting where the big pines had been cut. Interspersed stands of cedar, spruce, and small pine had been passed up as not fit for the lumber mills. Wildlife populations exploded in the new growth. Deer were everywhere. Rabbits and grouse abounded. Moose cruised the lowlands, feeding on new sprouts and boughs. With the rabbits came bobcats, lynx, and foxes. Residential communities of wolves, beavers, otters, martens, and fishers climbed toward peak numbers. A bounty on wolves offered a bonus for trappers, who could also market the thick gray pelts.

Word had gotten around Ely very early that some of the Northland's finest fishing could be found in the Knife Lake area. Busy guides took canoe groups on camping expeditions or made one-day trips from Berglund's Resort and the half dozen others already scattered down the Moose Chain and on Basswood Lake. Guides worked to establish reputations for ability and know-how in the wilderness—men like the Santineaus (Francis, John, and Jim); Vince and Joe Chosa; Hollis LaTourell; Martin Carlson; Gunnar Graves; and Bill Magie. Joe Chosa not only guided for Berglund but also regularly procured the resort's meat supply. This did not mean he shopped at Buccowich's Market in Ely. Like a lot of people living on the frontier, Berglund operated "out of the woods," and Joe shot a deer whenever the meat supply grew low. Those who hunted for meat did so discreetly, and no one discussed contraband meat publicly. But everyone who had stew at Berglund's, game wardens included, knew they were eating deer meat—and oftentimes, deer sausage, although much of that was made from legal deer taken the fall before.

Dorothy pitched in on the work load, sometimes guiding anglers up to Thunder Point, Birch Narrows, or the North Arm for trout. But more often she worked at the resort, keeping the cabins clean, the ice boxes filled, and the guests happy. She always kept on hand her small bird book, which she referred to whenever confronting an unknown species. Her natural curiosity took her on walks along the shorelines and inland to ridges, bogs, swamps, and streams, into the tall timber on the Canadian side and through the short new growth on the Minnesota shore. Because of the mix of old growth and new, the area held an unlimited variety of animal and bird life. From Joe Chosa, whom Dorothy fondly called "brother," she discovered the locations of several Native American burial grounds, but she soon learned not to show these to tourists, who were likely to rake over the sites, seeking "souvenirs."

Nightly sessions of card games in Berglund's cabin were embellished with stories by legendary Canadian rangers Bill Darby, Jack Powell, Art Madsen, and Jim Hendrickson. A fascinated Dorothy watched and listened at these gatherings, when glasses would clink, Bill's pipe would send up clouds of blue smoke, and tales, true and otherwise, would fill the cabin.

The cause may have been the trauma of losing her biological mother at an early age, or perhaps growing up with the job of caring for three younger children in the family, but Dorothy had no interest in the normally accepted goals set for young ladies in the 1930s. As she learned more about and came to love the vast wilderness on the U.S.–Canadian border, her ambition became to find a means of living in that country. Bill Berglund provided that means, that ticket to a life in the North. By 1933,

Dorothy had become a key member at the Isle of Pines operation, and in 1934 she moved north to stay.

Considerable concern arose in the Molter family over this headstrong daughter, who defied convention. A young woman of that era simply did not move in with a single man, not even one older than her own father. Dorothy attempted to explain to some members of her family that while she loved children and loved all her brothers and sisters, nephews and nieces, she clearly did not want children of her own. "Marriage is not for me," she declared. Her life, she said, lay in the Northland; while she might come home to visit, that was it.

Naturally, such a controversial attitude did not sit well with Cap, the tough disciplinarian, nor with Myrtle. Their relationship with Dorothy became strained and stayed strained for fifteen years. But Dorothy remained resolute. She knew what she wanted to do, knew what the costs were, accepted them, and set her sights on a new life. The people of the woods—the trappers, guides, Indians, game wardens, and their women— accepted her at face value as someone who could shoot, paddle, pack, or handle an ax with the best of them. Of course, some tuttutting occurred among a few members of the Ely and Winton social set, particularly among some of the early pillars of the churches, who were attempting to bring standards of moral behavior to a community that had been recently categorized by evangelist Billy Sunday as "one of the two worst places in creation . . . the other being Hell."

Dorothy, it turned out, had standards that were, in many respects, higher than those of her critics. Moreover, she had a tolerance for the vagaries of life and the failures of the human species. And she loved and cared for people, no matter what their situation. The break with life in Chicago was clean. With clear eyes and considerable courage, Dorothy began a new life on the northern frontier.

Living off the Land

From her Ojibwa friends, Dorothy often heard one of their traditional beliefs: "In the forest, the Great Spirit provides everything a person needs . . . we have only to understand how to use it."

Bill Berglund put it a little more pragmatically. "Dorothy," he pointed out, "there's no limit on the food in the forests—deer, moose, rabbits, grouse, and ducks—and fish from the waters. It doesn't take a whole lot of money to live in the woods if a person knows how to fish, hunt, and trap."

From the Chosas at Prairie Portage, Dorothy received her first supply of *manomin*, the staple grain of the Native People for centuries—wild rice. The Ojibwa harvested this cereal grain in late August or early September in Back Bay and Wind Bay of Basswood Lake, the Hula River, and Manomin Lake. Leo Chosa and his family and kinfolk regularly took hundreds of pounds by canoe and flail stick. The harvesters cured the rice in the sun until it turned black, then threshed it by placing it on a blanket or a clean deerskin and stamping on it with new

19

moccasins until the hulls broke loose from the kernels. Then they winnowed it—one person tossed it into the air from birchbark baskets or two people used a blanket, the wind carrying off the chaff, only pure grain remaining. This process, though lengthy and tedious, provided a highly nutritious cereal that could be bagged and kept for years. Dorothy learned how the Chosas cooked it as a vegetable dish, as a breakfast cereal, as a stuffing for wildfowl, or as an ingredient in soups and stews.

The area surrounding Knife Lake also abounded in berries. Hordes of tiny, brilliantly red strawberries, which could be made into preserves or served up with shortcake, ripened first. Raspberries flourished in the cutover areas, particularly on the sandy or graveled hillsides. These went into jams and jellies or sometimes cobblers for dessert. Blueberries grew plentifully on the cutover areas and on the islands up the lake. One of Bill's favorites was blueberry pie, either fresh from the bushes or in the winter from canned fruit. And few days went by without blueberry pancakes during berry season.

Other fruits grew in the area, too. Joe Chosa provided a reliable source of information on where to find the cranberry bogs and helped Dorothy identify Juneberries, or "saskatoons," found alongside portages and forest openings. Indian plums and the hips of wild roses went into other jams along with wild currants. Some summers, when a heavy crop of chokecherries appeared, Dorothy picked gallons from the dwarf trees and made them into a dark, tart jelly. In early spring, the emerging "fiddlehead" of the bracken fern furnished the ingredients for tasty salads over a period of weeks. Dorothy agreed—the Great Spirit provided well.

All spring, summer, and fall, trout, northern pike, and walleyes were a staple on the camp menu, along with an occasional snapping turtle, cut up and converted to soup. Then, in late fall, the serious fishing occurred. Bill took down the gill nets from their racks in the shed. He and Dorothy sat out in the sunshine, mending the mesh, testing the knots, adding new strands, until all was in readiness for cold weather. Toward the last of October, schools of large, flat-bodied whitefish moved into the shoreline shallows to spawn. And the nets were set. Dorothy and Bill ate some of the fish immediately, baked in the old wood stove. Some they brined and put through the smoking process, and some they salted and dried in the sun and crisp fall air. The lake's freezing over gave the signal to get out the ice-fishing equipment and set lines for trout or pike. Thus fish supplied protein year-round.

However, a most important part of their food supply was wild meat. Autumn changed the hillside thatch of birch and aspen from bright green to gold, punctuated by dark spires of spruce and fir, with the occasional flaming splash of a red or orange maple. The air had a sharpness, life quickened. Beavers cut more, jamming aspen and alder branches into the mud for their winter's food supply and enlarging their lodges with peeled saplings and grass—insulation against the coming cold. These changes marked the time to oil the guns and prepare for a new hunting season.

In the spring, and sometimes in the fall, the "drumming" sound of a male grouse beating his wings in rapid succession called a halt to all work momentarily, as Bill and Dorothy smiled knowingly. Bill quickly found out that Dorothy required no instruction and very little practice in shooting a .22 caliber rifle, the same type weapon with which she had won the City Championship while on her high school rifle team. Indeed, she was a better shot than Bill or any of his friends. Dorothy especially liked to toss the rifle in her canoe, pack a lunch, and head up the lake to hunt the portage trails where grouse often came out to feed, to preen, and to "dust."

"There was an accepted way of taking a grouse," she recalled. "It had to be picked off with a shot in the head. Anyone who came in with a grouse shot through the body—through the meat—had a lot of explaining to do, and would get a lot of kidding from the men around camp." At night, in the lantern-lit cabin, the aroma of grouse stuffed with wild rice emanated from the oven of the old wood stove. Sometimes golden brown grouse breasts were served up with tart wild cranberry sauce and then topped off with generous slices of blueberry pie, made from berries harvested in July. On these evenings, the hunting tales flew among Bill and his cronies, of days in the woods or on the water, seeking wildfowl. And the talk often turned to the coming deer season, that serious part of the year when hunters sought the winter's meat supply. Dorothy, always quiet in the background, hung on every word, absorbing the tales, savoring the atmosphere.

But before the deer, waterfowl could be hunted—some local nesters and some that came down from the North.

"Listen," Bill harked one morning, a hand cupped to one ear. "Geese!"

In the misty silence of an October dawn, the faint high clamor of Canadian honkers came, shrill, almost like the barking of small dogs. "There." Bill aimed a gnarled finger at the wedge of birds cruising overhead on slowly measured wingbeats, headed south in an ageless ritual. The time had come to get out the shotguns and paddle the canoe stealthily down the Knife River and through the weedy portions of Seed and Melon lakes, where mallards, black ducks, and teal could be stalked and bagged. They took turns at the paddling and shooting, both equally adept at dropping waterfowl winging up from the sedges and cattails in alarm. On Carp Lake, they sometimes pulled the canoe into the woods and hid behind shoreline brush, trying for fast-flying, black-and-white bluebills or white-bodied goldeneyes that flashed past. These ducks traveled low on the water in tight flocks, circling, landing, and taking off from mud flats below Knife Falls, where myriad tiny shellfish were found. Sometimes, when late fall trout fishermen came to camp, Dorothy baked up a half dozen mallards, stuffed with apples or carrots, basted with wine or brandy, and served them with steaming baked potatoes to men with appreciative palates and gargantuan appetites.

In late October, Bill and Dorothy ranged farther up the lake and back into the hills, both to check on the fur supply and to mark activity of whitetail deer. A supply of venison was considered a necessity for back-country living and was very nearly a staple of city life, too. During the 1930s, most of northern Minnesota existed largely on deer meat. Fortunately, as the Great Depression hit and unemployment rose, the deer population also expanded in the wake of logging, providing an easily acquired meat supply for most families. Cooks roasted, broiled, fried, smoked, and canned venison—and made it into sausage. To this day some old-timers will graciously decline an invitation to a venison supper, stating clearly that "we practically lived on that when I was growing up, and I can hardly stand to eat it any more."

"Just sitting in the woods with a rifle won't put any meat on the table," Bill often pointed out. "You've got to go where the deer are." And for that reason they hiked a lot, particularly the area between the Bonnie Lake and Spoon Lake portages, as well as the area along the south shore from Knife Lake to Birch. They sometimes checked out Robbins Island where, in some years, deer dwelt in good numbers. Those huge deer populations of the 1930s, 1940s, and later left a permanent mark on the countryside. In the winter, when the lakes were frozen, the animals followed the lake edges, feeding on shoreline cedar browse. In subsequent years, the deer ate the cedar leaves up as high as they could reach, even rearing up on hind legs. This created a "browse line," with green boughs above but no growth at all below. As time went on and deer populations went up and down, some shoreline cedar browse regenerated itself; however, summertime canoeists can still readily see that six-foot-high "browse line" of bare trunks and branches, created by the deer sixty years or more ago.

On their hikes to scout the deer country, Bill showed Dorothy how to read the signs. "See where that little balsam sapling is all skinned up? That's a rub mark where a buck polished his antlers, gettin' ready to fight for his does when the ruttin' season comes around.

"See where the ground is torn up there . . . where the leaves are all kicked away? That's called a scrape, where a buck stamped, and scuffed his hooves, markin' his territory. Wherever you find a lot of rubs and scrapes, those are good spots to hunt later on."

In many areas of the North, hunters went after deer as a group enterprise, with some of the best shots posted at strategic crossings and the other hunters forming a line to drive the deer into the shooters. But up on Knife Lake, deer hunting was pretty much solitary. Joe Chosa and other friends sometimes came up to inaugurate the season, but because the lakes might freeze at any time, there were never many hunters. Usually, the hunters went by boat or canoe to the mainland, each with a specific trail, or "run," selected as a good place to wait in ambush. Bill would drop Dorothy and some of the other hunters off along shore; if they hadn't scored by noon, they would hike to the boat, located at a prearranged point. If he heard some shots fired, Bill would come up with the boat and check to see if a deer was down and if the shooter needed help dragging it to the shore.

"Take your time," he advised Dorothy on deer hunting. "Make that first shot count. It can get to be an awful weary day if a buck is only wounded and has to be tracked over the hills and through the swamps."

Dorothy didn't need much advice on this score. When her .30-30 Winchester cracked, Bill knew she had her deer down and ready to be dressed out. Even though she was a trained nurse, she never cared for dressing out the deer. Dorothy never did develop a real killing instinct.

"I always felt kind of sorry for the deer," she confessed. "I knew we needed deer meat to get us through the winter, but

LIVING OFF THE LAND

they were such handsome animals with their grey coats, black muzzles, and white throats. It just about took my breath away every time I saw one approaching through the forest."

Each hunter carried a section of oilcloth in which to wrap the liver and heart, a necessity for an accepted table ritual with the first deer of each season. The liver was sliced crosswise, dipped in flour, fried up with onions, and then steamed under a cover until tender. The heart was boiled, chopped into pieces, and served up with gravy on buttered toast. The two interior fillets lying next to the backbone inside the body cavity were carefully washed in the lake, sliced across the grain, dusted in flour, and fried lightly in butter. Bill could never seem to get enough of these, his favorite delicacy.

Bill and Dorothy usually hung the deer carcasses to "age" during the deer season. By mid to late November, the weather turned cold and deer quarters could be stored inside one of the buildings, away from the bills of ravens and jays. Sometimes, they cut up a haunch and processed it for smoking, creating a delicious ham for the winter. And, if hunters from town came up by float plane, boned-out deer meat would be shipped back to town to be made up into deer sausage.

Sometimes, when Dorothy or Bill dispatched a particularly ornery old camp-raiding bear, they took off a shoulder roast, but usually they simply hauled the bear by boat over to the mainland and unceremoniously dumped it in the woods for other creatures to devour. Neither Bill nor Dorothy cared much for bear meat; it was greasy and the bears had a particularly unappetizing odor.

One year, in the middle 1940s, Bill got sick and required considerable care, so Dorothy didn't get much time to hunt. As a result, they went into the winter without their usual venison supply, a situation that grew critical as winter progressed and they used up their ducks, grouse, and fall-caught fish. Considerable deer hunting was still going on in the Knife Lake area, not by rifle-toting hunters but by wolves. On quiet nights, the wolf packs could be heard coursing through the hills, their long, mournful cries becoming an excited series of barks and howls as they closed in on their prey, and then a crescendo of wails as they brought down a deer and completed the kill. One night, listening to a pack hunting on the near shore, Dorothy and Bill heard the telltale cries of success. Bill grabbed a flashlight and a small sled, Dorothy the .30-30 Winchester, and they set off rapidly across the ice. The wolves had set up an ambush at a nearby point of land: one member of the pack lay in the snow, off the point, while the others drove the terrified deer out of the forest. The wolf in wait leaped, struck the deer on the neck, and dragged it to the snow. The successful hunters gathered, pointed their muzzles skyward, and signaled with their cry of success.

As they hurried toward the kill, Dorothy fired a rifle shot, dispersing the pack, which "lit out for the woods like the devil was chasing them."

"The wolves had ripped open the body cavity," Dorothy recalled, "and had eaten the heart, liver, and lungs . . . but most of the meat was intact. We cut off the hind quarters and the two back loins, loaded up the sled and headed home."

Dorothy remembered the episode with a chuckle. "That was some of the best deer meat we ever had . . . maybe because we got it from the wolves. And we didn't feel bad about hijacking it . . . we knew they would get more as soon as they came back and cleaned up the front quarters.

"Shucks, there were lots of deer," she added. "Some years, the wolves killed more than they could eat and left carcasses along the shoreline, just ripping the deer open and eating the insides. The ravens and foxes usually made short work of the rest . . . and some years there would be an eagle or two still around . . . and they would share in the wolf kills, too.

"You can't believe how fast ravens can clean up a dead deer. Hungry wolves will sometimes eat the whole works, right down to the feet, but usually there are some parts left on the ice . . . often the ribs and back. Maybe thirty or forty ravens would cluster on top of the deer's remains, squawking and yawping and picking away until there wasn't anything left but part of the skeleton and some hair."

Tough times came to Knife Lake during the 1940s. The resort business fell off sharply during the war years, when gas rationing curtailed travel. Bill became less able to get around; in 1944 he had a bad fall and broke his arm, and he already suffered from diabetes, kidney disease, and heart problems. Dorothy had almost a full-time job as nurse. When Bill finally got so weak he required hospital care, Dorothy packed him to Moose Lake, from where he was taken to the hospital in Virginia. He died on March 22, 1948, at age seventy-four.

Dorothy, a young and vigorous forty-one, strong and capable, was determined to go back to Knife Lake and live out her life. Bill had said for years that he had willed the property to Dorothy. There was just one thing wrong: Bill left no will. Title to the property automatically went to his brother and sister. It was an incredible letdown for Dorothy. Her heart and soul were at Isle of Pines, where she had labored for fifteen years. All of the hard work, all of the time spent with the ailing man, appeared to go the way of empty promises.

But Bill's brother and sister, August Berglund of St. Hilaire, Minnesota, and Mrs. Kate Johnson of Vashon Island, Washington, were well aware of Dorothy's sacrifice and dedication, and they were uncommon people. How much the resort would have brought if advertised on the real estate market is difficult to reckon, but it would have been many thousands of dollars. But the brother and sister quietly met at the Lake County Court House in Two Harbors and had the property deeded over to Dorothy. In that simple but generous gesture, they honored Bill's wishes and provided a lifetime legacy for Dorothy Molter. The move also helped to reconcile Dorothy with her family, particularly her dad, whose visits had tailed off. Cap resumed his fishing trips and began to spend more time at the island, summer and winter. Other members of the family came up more often—sisters, brothers, nieces, nephews. And Dorothy resumed regular visits to Chicago. During the years she lived with Bill, she very seldom ventured out of the Ely area, and she told more than one reporter she "had not seen a big-city Christmas in fourteen years." Now Dorothy still lived off the land, but a new era had begun.

Nightingale
of the Wilderness

IT DOES NOT TAKE LONG for the North Woods "moccasin tele-graph" to carry news, particularly news of a helpful nature. Even in the remote area of Knife Lake, the word got around that the young lady at Isle of Pines was a trained registered nurse. And in such a remote setting, where medical assistance is often hard to come by, Dorothy Molter became a vital asset among those who carved out a livelihood in the canoe country as well as among those who simply passed through on their summer canoe trips.

No one really knows who first called Dorothy the "Florence Nightingale of the Wilderness," named after the famed English nurse who led a staff of thirty-eight volunteer women into the screaming horror of the Crimean War in 1854, the first women nurses to attend battlefield wounded. But the name caught on in the border lakes country.

"Florence Nightingale," however, turned out to be too big a

31

mouthful for the more tight-lipped Northlanders, who conse-
quently shortened it to "Nightingale of the Wilderness." At
times this caused some confusion among nonresident visitors,
who thought the comely resident of Knife Lake might somehow entertain passing canoeists with an assortment of songs or
bird calls. However, people who lived in Winton and Ely, as
well as paddlers traveling the canoe routes, quickly found her
medical talents valuable in times of distress.

As the canoe outfitting industry expanded, outfitters map-
ping trips through the Knife Lake area always advised their
clients: "If you get into real trouble, an injury or something,
head for Isle of Pines at the eastern part of Knife Lake and
Dorothy will provide help."

Among the first friends Dorothy made along the border
lakes were the Chosas, native Ojibwas whose ancestors had
lived on Basswood Lake for centuries. Leo Chosa had a small
resort, bait business, store, and boat trailer operation at Prairie
Portage, where the Knife River boomed down over an old
logging dam and a series of falls. Anglers wishing to get their
boats carried from the Moose Chain into Basswood could, for
a small fee, have Leo haul their craft the quarter mile around the
dam and falls. Often, when returning from a supply run to Ely,
Dorothy would swing her loaded canoe into Leo's dock and
walk down to his cabin for a cup of coffee and the latest gossip
on the lake. He had a recurring eye problem that Dorothy
ministered to, but it wasn't his eye that brought her down once
in the middle of winter.

The nurse really wasn't surprised one early forty-below-zero
morning in 1951 when the engine on bush pilot Hoot Hautala's
Stinson monoplane set Dorothy's red cocker spaniel Peg to
barking. Jamming a pair of jeans on over her pajamas and
donning a wool jacket, Dorothy ran with Peg down to the
lakeshore as Hoot's plane made a second pass. Seeing Dorothy,
he leaned out of the cockpit and hurled a tin can into the snow,
then banked away and circled slowly. Dorothy retrieved the

can, pulled out a slip of paper from inside and read: "LEO'S BACK NO BETTER. ICE TOO ROUGH. CAN'T LAND ELY DOCTOR THERE. CAN YOU LOOK AT IT?"

Dorothy stamped out a big "YES" in the snow and waved as Hoot hit the throttle and aimed the nose of his craft for Ely. She had planned to snowshoe into town that week for an appointment with the dentist. The problem at Leo's meant she would just go a couple of days early.

Dorothy hurried inside the cabin and began preparations to leave. The bird feeder outside the kitchen window had to be stocked with seeds and bits of corn bread for the chickadees, jays, and nuthatches. She put out chunks of deer suet for the woodpeckers. The kerosene lantern was filled in readiness for a possible return after dark and a couple armloads of kindling were stacked in the box next to the stove. She shouldered her packsack with first-aid supplies, added a couple of sandwiches and some biscuits for the cocker spaniel, and started out the door. At the lakeshore she paused to push her way through the three doorways into the dirt-covered root cellar, lit a couple of candles as a frost-preventive measure, then strapped on her snowshoes and headed west.

Ordinarily, Dorothy wore jeans, plaid shirt, wool socks, and sneakers. For the trip to Leo's, she left the pajamas underneath and added a wool jacket, overshoes over the sneakers, and wool-lined leather mittens on her hands. As usual, she wore no hat, her hair more or less held in place by a band across the top. Although dressed relatively lightly for the bitter cold, she knew that the exertion from snowshoeing would keep her comfortably warm.

Her breath and Peg's drifted in white clouds across the unbroken snow as they trekked down to the Melon Lake portage, hugged the shoreline to avoid thin ice by the rapids, and crossed down to Seed Lake. Dorothy gave the treacherous currents and dangerous ice at both Knife Falls and Carp Falls a wide berth. Then she had a clear surface for four more miles to

Prairie Portage. It had been 7:30 when she left the cabin on Knife, and it took five hours of steady walking before she unstrapped her snowshoes and stepped through the doorway of Leo's cabin, pulling off her mittens and jacket.

In addition to a sprained back, acquired when he had slipped on the ice below the falls at Prairie Portage, Leo had cracked a bone in his wrist. Between sips of hot coffee provided by Leo's wife, Dorothy splinted the wrist and then instructed the thick-set Ojibwa to soak his back regularly with an Epsom salt solution as hot as he could stand. In addition, she gave him a thorough tongue-lashing for engaging in rough physical work, which had prevented his back from healing. She ordered him to bed and told his wife to see that he stayed there until the pain subsided. With that, she strapped on her snowshoes and headed for her destination on Moose Lake, six miles farther west.

It had been relatively easy and quiet walking on the way down in the crisp morning. The only sound other than the rhythmic swish-swish of her snowshoes was the occasional boom of ice thickening and expanding on the lake surfaces. It had warmed slightly since dawn, but the temperature still stood below zero as Dorothy and Peg trudged along. And then they ran into pockets of dreaded slush. Those not familiar with North Country lakes cannot comprehend "slush," huge areas of mixed water and snow that remain unfrozen even with temperatures in the minus thirties and forties. Snow presses the ice downward, forcing warmer lake water up through fissures in the surface. This water spreads out over the ice but beneath the snow cover, effectively insulated from freezing. Slush remains unfrozen, from several inches to a foot thick, for days or even weeks. At times the snow crusts over slightly, but winter travelers can unwittingly break through into mushy snow and water up to their boot tops or even over.

Dorothy snowshoed into just such slush coming down Sucker Lake. As her snowshoes went through the crust, into the slop, and then up into the subzero air, her feet became encased in balls of ice the size of two watermelons. She could do nothing but flounder to shore and then beat the snowshoe bindings with a stick until she could free her boots. Then she took off the snowshoes and hit the frames and webbing, chipping off the ice but taking care not to crack the ash frames or break the rawhide. Peg sat in the snow, chewing balls of ice from her legs and from the hair between her toes. Once they were both ice-free, Dorothy strapped the snowshoes back on and took off.

Halfway down Newfound Lake, they floundered into another hidden slush trap; this time Dorothy went in over the tops of her overshoes. With ice water sloshing inside her boots, she headed shoreward, once again accumulating huge, icy balls around her feet. While Peg whined and tugged at her ice-matted hair, Dorothy kindled a small fire, dumped the water out of her boots, dried her socks somewhat, and prepared to move on. She first had to beat the ice again from the snowshoe frames and webbing. Dorothy knew from experience that if she attempted to melt the ice from the webbing the rawhide would become soft and soggy, and make walking difficult.

Darkness came, and they were still far from Moose Lake, but they plodded onward, growing more bone-weary from wading through one slush hole after another. Dorothy fought off any inclination to stop and rest, recalling woods-wise Bill Berglund's terse admonition: "Stop and you freeze to death. Keep walking and you live."

It was 9 P.M., four and one-half hours after sunset, when she spotted the lights of Canadian Border Lodge, stumbled up the path, and banged on the door. It had taken Peg and her almost fourteen hours to traverse the fourteen miles from Knife Lake, twice the normal trip length. The trip to the dentist the next day was almost a relief.

Dorothy's first-aid efforts at Knife Lake encompassed a wide variety of traumas. Once she set a broken ankle and fashioned a set of crutches out of saplings for an injured canoeist, who then hung around until his leg got strong enough to travel.

NIGHTINGALE OF THE WILDERNESS

Twice she administered first aid to campers who had been stunned and burned when lightning struck near their tents. In one instance, involving a man and his son who were subsequently flown out, doctors in Ely said Dorothy's first-aid treatment had probably saved their lives. But most cases were not severe: burns from pans left on a hot fire, stomach cramps from a bit of soap carelessly left inside a cook pot, errant fishhooks buried in the flesh, or cuts from knives or axes.

Once two boys paddled into camp, one with a badly slashed foot from contact with a sharp rock. Dorothy, who did not have any anesthetic at camp, told the injured paddler, "This is going to hurt a little" to get sewed up. A dentist camping on a nearby island happened to stop by for a cold root beer, and Dorothy drafted him as an assistant. With Cap and the canoeist's buddy helping the dentist hold the howling boy down, Dorothy washed out the wound, dusted it with sulfa drugs, and stitched it up.

And there was the time a despondent woman on the island tried to commit suicide by swallowing a fistful of sleeping pills. Dorothy immediately went into action, emptying out the woman's system with strong coffee enemas, placing ice packs on her head, and walking her around for the balance of the day and all night. By the next morning, the woman had recovered and, after some sympathetic but firm counseling from the wilderness nurse, decided that maybe life was worth living after all.

Not only did Dorothy provide medical help, but she sometimes mended the spirit as well. Late one fall, canoeing alone down Birch Lake on her way to town for supplies, she spotted a small tent with a canoe pulled up, but no one apparently around. Curious, she put into shore and found a rather despondent young man who had just suffered through a nerve-wracking divorce and had "gone off into the wilderness" to pitch camp, put out a few traps, and try to pull together the raveled shreds of his life.

It took only minutes for Dorothy to get the young man talking. As he mumbled his sad tale, she realized that his chances of surviving the oncoming winter in a canvas tent were next to nil. Pointing out that she could use another strong back and an extra pair of arms up at her camp, she invited him to come up and use one of her cabins. She said she would stop by his camp on the return trip and he could follow her back. Furthermore, she noted, he'd find a lot more beaver and other furbearers up around Knife Lake than where he was presently camped.

The young man, Jim Keil, did move up to the Isle of Pines for the winter. He managed to dissipate his sadness in the healing atmosphere of the wilderness, bolstered by some of Dorothy's venison stew, and had a successful trapping season. He came out in the spring with 105 beaver pelts.

During the following summer, Jim worked at resorts in the area, then did some more trapping around Knife Lake, splitting wood and handling some of Dorothy's heavier camp chores. To acquaintances, Jim admitted he had hit absolute rock bottom when Dorothy stopped by his tent on Birch Lake, and the time spent with Dorothy had been incredible therapy. They became staunch friends; and when Jim later moved north to try trapping in Alaska, he regularly wrote Dorothy and inquired as to how things were at Isle of Pines.

Not all of Dorothy's medical work involved people. She doctored any number of birds and small animals brought to her cabin with a variety of ailments, and once she handled a major injury to Bill Berglund's pet dog, Nebs. Normally a big, easygoing, half-Alaskan husky and half-shepherd, Nebs had one fault. He barked at airplanes and hated the droning machines that taxied up to the dock on floats. One day his anger overcame his better judgment, and with teeth bared, he charged an approaching plane. As Nebs darted off the dock and onto a pontoon, the whirling propeller caught him in the head and knocked him flying into the lake. Pulled out in a bloody mess, he obviously had a smashed jaw. The pilot suggested they shoot him and end his misery, but after Nebs gave Dorothy a long, sad look she carried him into the cabin, cleaned off the blood, and set the jaw, anchoring it in place with a birchbark splint. The jaw, she admitted, grew back a little crooked, but she fed him soup and milk until he got well. "One thing about old crooked-jaw Nebs," Dorothy recalled, "he never chased another float plane as long as he lived."

Probably the most trying nursing tasks that confronted Dorothy came when she helped Bill Berglund as the woodsman's health began failing in the late 1930s and early 1940s. It seemed impossible that this self-sufficient, strong-hearted man of the forest could become sick, but he began to suffer from a series of ailments, including heart disease and kidney infections. In the winter of 1940, Bill became critically ill at the cabin. In spite of his weak protests, Dorothy determined that he required quick medical help and hospitalization. Although a blizzard was raging outside, she rolled him up in a sleeping bag, lashed him to a toboggan, and set out for Ely on snowshoes.

"It was hard work pulling that load through the deep snow," Dorothy recalled. "And it was hard to keep track of the trail in that blizzard." Moving a lot slower than she intended, they were caught by darkness as they entered Ensign Lake. Deciding they had to get out of the weather, she pulled the toboggan to an old trapper's line shack on the lake and groped her way inside. The shack had lost its window and the door had long fallen off the hinges, but she found an old barrel stove still intact inside, and a rusted iron bed frame stood in the corner. Kindling a fire, she shoved the bed frame up against the stove, untied Bill from the toboggan, and slid him onto the frame next to the stove. Then she lay next to him on the outside, sheltering him from the snow-laden wind swirling in through the doorway.

At first light, she was up and going. Bill was less than conscious as she again lashed him inside his sleeping bag to the toboggan. The storm had lifted and visibility was better as she lit out for Moose Lake on her snowshoes.

"It was about noon when I got to Canadian Border Lodge," she said. "There wasn't anybody around . . . they had left. But the door was open, so I pulled Bill into the main lodge, got a fire going, and rang up Ely on the old crank phone." After a couple of buzzes, she got the operator and informed her that there was an emergency out at the lodge. The operator notified a sheriff's deputy and within the hour Bill was on his way to the Ely hospital.

"He was in there for some time, but they took care of him OK," Dorothy recalled. "But it was sure a scary trip." Bill survived to spend several more seasons at his beloved Isle of Pines.

Not only was Dorothy's medical help important to many wilderness folk over the years, but her assistance in rescue work was vital. As her fame with tape and bandage became legendary, canoe outfitters regularly marked paddler's maps with a dot and the name "Dorothy," informing their clients that in the event of a real emergency, her cabin served as a way station for rescue. While most of her visitors stopped by for a cold root beer or a couple of candy bars, a considerable number came in with injuries, some of which required more advanced treatment. In those cases, Dorothy would administer whatever first aid she could, then race down to the dock at the sound of an approaching float plane and wave a towel to signal the pilot. No matter if it was a flying game warden, Forest Service patrol plane, or bush pilot hauling supplies or people, the pilot always made an accommodation to provide emergency airborne ambulance service to town.

Justly proud of her medical treatment in the back country, Dorothy left a notice in her will that said when she was buried, she wanted her stone to read simply: "Nightingale of the Wilderness."

Winter the Hard Way

GENERATIONS OF HARDY RESIDENTS have described the Northland as a place "where you have nine months of winter and three months of tough sledding." This obvious exaggeration elicits plenty of laughs from summer visitors and local folk alike, but the truth is that northern Minnesota has a lot more winter than summer. Snowfall is common in October, serious in November; and what falls by Thanksgiving usually stays around until the following April or May, albeit buried under several more feet of accumulated drifts. Sometimes the snow lasts up to June in isolated clumps back among the moss in shady nooks where the sun does not hit, providing spring trout anglers with built-in natural iceboxes in which to store their fish. Dorothy moved into the winter aspect of the North in 1934. Before that, she had listened to a lot of yarns about the winters in the North, some true, some stretched beyond comprehension. One tall tale told about lumberjacks swearing up a blue stream in mid-January, the words freezing in the air, only to thaw out in the spring and suddenly assault the hearing of unsuspecting canoe paddlers passing by. In a true story, a logger died of a heart attack in the woods near Ely, where his companions found him sitting frozen against a tree. They put him on a horse-drawn logging wagon, hauled him to camp, and the following Saturday took him to town. On the way down Sheridan Street to the mortuary, they decided to pause for a warming, 90-proof "bump" at a local pub, tied up the horses, and prepared to go inside. At this point, one of the lumberjacks, out of consideration for their departed comrade, suggested that they "take Old Fritz inside with us for one last drink." Since Fritz had frozen in a sitting position, it was quite easy to haul him through the door and quietly set him up in a chair by their table. All the rest sat around, ordering their drinks, and also a "shot and a beer" for Fritz, who just sat quietly staring ahead. The place was packed, but no one paid any particular attention to the one very rigid "drinker," whom his pals naturally included in the conversation at the table. When the 'jacks had consumed their drinks and felt properly fortified against the wintry elements, they paid their bill, picked up their rigid friend, and carried him back to the wagon for the final ride to the undertaker's. Considerable hilarity followed in the logging camp over this somewhat irreverent prank, and eventually the story got around Ely. Old-timers still relate this favorite yarn about the logger who was "already stiff" when they took him into the saloon.

Dorothy, ever the history buff and frontier romanticist, hung on every word of these tales, devouring and memorizing them to tell later. However, she tended to keep in the background when the men told stories. Townsfolk remember the demure young woman as extremely shy in those early days, partly because of gossip concerning her relationship with Bill Berglund.

But how Dorothy loved to hear about the real people, men like old-time game wardens Bill Hansen and the Ojibwa John Linklater, who operated in the winter by dog sled from the old fish and game headquarters in Winton. Bill Berglund had worked with Hansen and Linklater and could roll off unending tales of these two, whom he held in high esteem. And there were the trappers who came into Vertin's Restaurant for a big steak dinner with the trimmings when they first came out of the woods with their sled loads of pelts. Men like John Sansted and Al Johnson of Winton would head out on snowshoes in the dead of winter with their traps and perhaps a light tent lashed to a toboggan. They would live alone for weeks at a time in the sub-zero cold, existing mainly on meat they shot or trapped, bolstered by beans and bannock.

These men spun endless yarns of close calls in the wilderness, of falling through the ice and working with their heads underwater to release their snowshoes so they could crawl out. They sometimes carried sharpened spikes driven into two cylinders of wood. These they hung around their necks on thongs, tools that they could jab into the ice to pull themselves out of a hole if they fell through.

Some of the stories, told in hushed voices, concerned trappers they knew who had accidents and didn't make it out, men who were found dead in the woods—or some who were never found at all. Stories of lost souls whose spirits still roamed the wilderness were told by old men who claimed to have heard their cries in the night. These tales and the excitement of living in the wilderness in the winter drew Dorothy north for good. She had an incredible opportunity to learn about this remote, wild country, its animals, its birds, and the people who survived in it.

And Bill Berglund was a skilled instructor. He knew the Knife Lake country like city people know their back yards. Bill not only had patrolled it as a game warden, he trapped and hunted the area and had worked in the winter as a timber cutter. Winters to the hardy Finn merely meant a change in travel mode, from canoe to snowshoes. To him, the wilderness even at forty below was a very likable and livable place. "Winter," he opined, "is the best time of the year to be in the woods because there are no blackflies or mosquitoes."

Their first winter trips together came during the trapping season. Dorothy learned how to break trail on snowshoes, spelling Bill off every few hundred yards, noting how much easier it was to move when one snowshoer had already gone ahead. They snowshoed from Moose Lake to Knife, each pulling a toboggan with supplies, packing a trail that they could then follow more easily coming back down later. Dorothy learned how to build a lunch fire by first laying a platform of branches on the snow, then making the fire on that. She found out how to set up "back logs" against poles jammed into the snow, logs that would not only burn but reflect the heat forward. She learned that the open summer campsites, situated to catch the breeze, became worthless in the winter and that one made camp back in the shelter of a cedar or spruce swamp where the bitter wind could not reach.

Bill kept his traps, fur stretchers, and trail equipment at Isle of Pines, so they had to pack in only supplies for immediate use. Like all woodsmen, Bill was essentially a meat eater.

"I never in my life saw people eat meat like those guys," Dorothy remarked. "They ate deer meat, moose meat, beaver, rabbits—about everything except skunk and they would probably have eaten that if they got hungry enough." Moose, of course, were protected by law, and any available moose meat was contraband. Still, some people had it, and folks jokingly referred to it as "Canadian beef." Leo Chosa and his family at Basswood Lake occasionally had moose. Joe Chosa, whom Bill called "Injun Joe," and Leo's son Vincent, were trappers and hunters like their Ojibwa ancestors, and essentially meat eaters. Sometimes Joe came up to run traps and hunt with Bill, whom he held in high esteem.

Dorothy recalled one time she and Bill went snowshoeing down for a visit to Leo's cabin at Prairie Portage; partway there, she spied what looked like two stumps in the snow ahead. "Only the stumps seemed to be moving a little, and I pointed this out to Bill. At first he thought they might be wolves and brought his rifle up, but then decided they weren't." The "stumps" turned out to be Canadian Ranger Bob Halliday and his trail partner, who were brewing up a pot of tea.

Dorothy and Bill shared their sandwiches with the Canadians, who inquired as to what kind of meat was between the slices of bread.

"Canadian beef," Bill said, and the two Canadians roared.

"They never said anything about having a problem eating illegal moose meat," Dorothy remembered.

When Bill and Dorothy were not up at Knife Lake, they lived in Winton. Bill roomed for awhile with the Ballinger family, then got a house of his own. Dorothy roomed with the Carpenters, according to some local historians. Ellen Hansen, wife of game warden Bill Hansen, recalled that Bill was not only a good woodsman but an inveterate gambler, a poker player. His house became the winter gathering point for most of Winton's card-playing gentry, one of them being J. C. Russel, the postmaster and also chief clerk for the Swallow & Hopkins Lumber Company.

"Those poker games sometimes ran on all night and all day," Ellen recalled. "Whenever somebody needed the postmaster and couldn't find him, they went down to Bill's house and usually found him there deep into a game."

During the years from 1934 to 1948, Chicago-raised Dorothy became adapted to life in the wilderness. And she learned. She was forever learning: how to hunt deer; how to snowshoe; how to read the hundreds of stories, the triumphs and tragedies, in tracks and imprints left on the snow. She could tell from a few wisps of hair and a spot of blood where a great horned owl feasted on an unwary rabbit. From scales on the ice, she marked where an otter brought up a northern pike for dinner. And often patches of deer hair, hooves, and antlers, sometimes parts of carcasses, showed where a wolf pack had completed a successful stalk. The eerie howl of wolf packs on the hunt, echoing across the hills surrounding Knife Lake, regularly broke the silence of the night. On one trip to town, Dorothy said, they counted fourteen deer carcasses or parts of them, all wolf kills.

During the spring beaver trapping season, Knife Lake became sort of a crossroads for trappers, game wardens, and ice fishermen coming in by ski-equipped planes. They all considered Isle of Pines a haven from the harsh weather. Dorothy cooked up mammoth pots of venison stew and the men stuffed themselves, spun yarns, and played poker until the wee hours, quite often killing a bottle of whiskey in the process. Sometimes, when the glasses were clinking and the stories flying, the subject matter became somewhat ribald. "When that happened," Dorothy said, "Bill would look around at me and say it was time for me to get to bed. He didn't like for me to hear all the rough talk and swearing."

From 1940 onward, Bill was more often ailing and their winter trips became increasingly difficult. More and more, Bill depended on Dorothy to handle the chores, cut the wood, and keep the fire going. Tough, and resilient, she learned the woods, came to appreciate the ways of the wilderness, both winter and summer. When Bill died in 1948, she had more than a decade of experience and knowledge, which helped her immeasurably when she decided to stay at Knife Lake alone. Alone, that is, except for those same trappers, game wardens, and ice fishermen, who still headed for the cabin on Isle of Pines. The poker games faded away, but the venison stew still bubbled on the stove and the colorful stories went on as before, except perhaps on a somewhat less profane level.

"I kept a bottle of my own around there in those days," Dorothy recalled, "for the guys in case they wanted a nip to ward off the cold. But I found out that they weren't satisfied with one nip. If I got the bottle out, they wanted to finish it, and usually did. So I quit stocking whiskey for those guys. They either brought their own or drank coffee."

The Winton gossip circuit included considerable conjecture about "that young woman living all alone up there in the winter," with some worrying that she could readily be the target of someone's evil pursuits. But it didn't happen. First, the men who came through there, no matter how high or low their level of morality, seemed to have a special, almost mystical, respect for Dorothy. On the other hand, none but a fool would have made a move on her because the others would have hunted him down. She generated that kind of loyalty. Furthermore, every one of those winter visitors knew that their hostess was a dead shot with a rifle, and a very powerful woman, probably physically stronger that nine out of ten men. She could swing a splitting ax with considerable authority—and probably swing a haymaker just as well. No doubt, a few liquored-up jackpine savages toyed with the idea of invading Dorothy's bedroom but thought better of it, realizing, even in their bleary condition, that they would be lucky to escape intact.

After Bill's death Dorothy began taking more trips back to Chicago and to other parts of the country to visit relatives on a regular basis. This forged closer ties with her family, and she could also once again participate in the colorful holiday seasons in the city, which she thoroughly enjoyed. On those trips she worked at the Auburn Park Hospital (which came to be called St. George's). The resort never brought her more than a meager income, and Dorothy depended on her hospital work to bolster her personal treasury. Nursing work provided funds for the multitude of gifts she always distributed among the family members. She also needed supplies for the resort, and by working double shifts—not particularly strenuous for someone with her stamina—she could put together a fair nest egg over several weeks.

Dorothy used Anderson's Resort on Moose Lake as sort of an access and headquarters for trips in and out. The resort lodge, according to records, had been one of the main logging camps of Swallow and Hopkins. Bill and Wanda Anderson operated the resort and loved to tell stories of the old days. Wanda remembers Dorothy as extremely shy; but slowly, she became warm friends with the Andersons, and sometimes snowshoed down in early winter, always bringing some sort of a toy for their small child, Robin.

"Dorothy would tell Robin that Santa Claus always made an early 'test run' through Knife Lake before Christmas," Wanda remembers, "just to see if it would be OK to come down later with his whole team of reindeer—and that Santa had dropped off the toy for Dorothy to deliver to Robin.

"We used to sit around the kitchen table drinking coffee together. One time I came right out and asked Dorothy why she didn't get married. Dorothy looked me in the eye and said: 'When I find a guy who can paddle better, shoot straighter, snowshoe faster, split wood quicker, and portage bigger loads, I'll marry him.' That pretty well ended the speculation."

In the 1950s, Northland winters began to change from snowshoes and dog sleds to gasoline engines. In part, the change came because servicemen from World War II had acquired a background in military vehicles and mechanics and an inclination to apply this knowledge to the outdoors.

Duluthian Dick Abrahamson and his buddies, Dick James and Bob Zapolski, built "wind sleds," small, closed-in vehicles on runners, driven by airplane propellers. Dick purchased a sixty-five-horsepower Continental engine salvaged from a plane that dove into Silver Lake, near Virginia. Expert with machinery, he restored the engine to top-notch working order, picked up a prop for it, and built it into a conduit-framed, aluminum-covered sled on skis.

"The completed sled weighed between five hundred and six hundred pounds," Dick said. "On a warm day, when there was soft snow, it would travel about thirty miles per hour; but when it was cold, the surface packed and hard, it would do seventy on an open stretch."

The sleds owned by Abrahamson, James, and Zapolski were four-seaters but normally ran with two, the rear section used for storage. "When we went up to Dorothy's," Abrahamson noted, "we put pieces of plywood behind the front seats like partitions and filled the back of the sled with supplies."

One of their objectives in traveling up to Dorothy's in the winter, other than to do some trout fishing, was to help her put up ice for the following summer. In short order, they got tired of hand-cutting the ice and set about devising a better system. "We modified an old David Bradley gasoline-powered wood saw," Dick recalled, "which could be skidded out on the ice and used to saw down, but not quite through the ice surface. This way, the ice was scored in blocks and could then be finished up with a hand saw or simply broken loose with an ice chisel."

Dorothy enjoyed riding in the wind sleds, and so did Cap, who took to coming up in the winter after Bill died. "Sometimes we ran them up in the spring," said Dick, "when there was water on top of the ice. They got a kick out of seeing the big rooster tails of water spraying out in back."

For several winters, Dick and his friends came up right after freeze-up to pick up Dorothy, giving her a ride out to Moose Lake for any shopping she needed to do in Ely. "One time I had mechanical problems with the sled," he said laughing, "and I was a whole day late going in. I got an early start but when I got to her cabin, Cap was there and said she had left the night before. Then I saw her snowshoe tracks and realized she had headed down the lake, walking out."

He followed her tracks right to Wanda Anderson's, where she was inside having coffee. "She said she waited most of the day before and when she realized I wasn't coming, simply walked out. When she saw me starting out the next morning, she ran out on Wanda's dock and tried to signal me with a mirror, reflecting the sun, but I just went steaming right past. She laughed and wanted to know if my eyesight was failing."

Hollis LaTourell noticed some ingenious winter travelers beginning to experiment with tracked snow sleds, and he convinced Dorothy that she ought to have one built, a sled that would be a lot better for hauling supplies and that could be used to get Cap in and out more easily. Hollis knew of two top-notch machinists in Hinckley—Chester Maser and his partner Donald DuPre—and convinced them to build Dorothy a machine. He made a rough sketch of what was needed and contracted for the vehicle at $800, a considerable sum at that time.

"We didn't even know if we could build such a machine," Maser recalled. "But we started out with a two-cycle, twelve-horse Ohman gas engine. We hooked it up to a three-speed Chevrolet transmission, but we couldn't find a clutch that would work, so we made one in our machine shop. The track was a section of rubber belt from an old gravel conveyor. It had chains on both sides. When we got it done, it must have weighed a thousand pounds."

It took the two men two months, working nights after supper, to complete the machine. Hollis drove down with a truck in the early spring and hauled it out to Moose Lake. He then drove it up to Dorothy's. It was the first "snowmobile" anyone around there had ever seen, the first of what would become fleets of machines in a few short years. The sturdy vehicle proved its worth over many seasons; but because of its weight, it sometimes seemed to be almost more trouble than it was worth. On good, packed snow, it performed excellently, but perfect conditions seldom appear in the Northland. Lightness had been sacrificed for strength, and at the first pocket of slush the sled bogged down. When it got buried in slush, two people had to do a lot of prying, pushing, and pulling to get it free. It was so wide, it would sometimes get hung up on a stump or rock. And, in some situations, that Ohman engine just quit. Dorothy got to be fairly expert at diagnosing mechanical problems and fixing them. Very often she came down to Moose Lake with grease up to her elbows, vowing that the snowmobile would never replace a sturdy set of legs on snowshoes. However, Cap loved it and considered it a vital piece of equipment. Cap simply didn't have the legs to snowshoe four miles, much less fourteen, and the snowmobile provided the means to get him in and out of Knife Lake. But it wasn't always simple.

One winter, Cap and Dorothy headed for Ely with two toboggans in tow, intending to pick up a pair of hundred-pound bottled gas tanks and some fresh vegetables, plus the mail. As Dorothy told it later: "Things went fine until we got to Vera Lake and the motor stalled. After about an hour we got it going again, but when we reached Ensign Lake, it stalled once more. We coaxed and cussed and fumed and finally got the sled on the way but it only lasted one mile.

"Cap and I took the motor apart and put it together, keeping warm by pulling on the starter cord, over and over again. We had lost a lot of time and it was getting late. Not only that, but it was beginning to snow pretty hard and the wind was blowing.

"I told Cap that if we got the engine going, we had better turn back because we couldn't tell what kind of ice conditions we might meet ahead in the dark. Eventually, we got it running and made it back to Knife Lake. In the next couple of days, Cap figured out the trouble and so we left again for Moose Lake."

This time they made it without any problems. They picked up the two tanks of bottled gas, put one on each toboggan, hooked up in tandem, and started back. Halfway over the first portage, from Newfound through the woods to Splash Lake, the machine lost traction and wouldn't pull. So they untied the toboggans and Cap took the machine over while Dorothy pulled the two toboggans across by hand, one at a time.

From there, they made it up to the end of Ensign, where it started all over again. Dorothy pulled one toboggan over to Vera Lake while Cap ran the snow sled across. The Vera portage has some steep spots in it, and the footing was so bad she had to leave the second toboggan. Besides, Dorothy noticed they were running low on fuel and thought it best to get to the cabin as soon as possible.

"Well, wouldn't you know it," Dorothy said, "We ran out of gas going from Portage Lake to Knife. Cap couldn't walk in the snow with his bad legs, but I had my snowshoes strapped to the sled for emergencies, so I untied them, put them on, and crossed over the bay to the cabin. Cap made a fire on the shore to keep warm until I returned. I really rushed to get back with the extra can of gasoline, making the round trip in 40 minutes. We filled the tank, got the machine going and made it to the cabin OK."

Two days later they went back and managed to haul the toboggans with the gas tanks to the cabin. "That sled could be a wonderful thing, but the snow had to be just right," she observed later.

One early spring, when Cap was back in Chicago, an unseasonable thaw made traveling nearly impossible on the snow sled. Dorothy waited and watched but it didn't get colder. Instead, it got warmer, and the ice began pulling away from the shore in places. The April 15 deadline for filing income tax returns came and went, and Dorothy still couldn't get to town on the snowmobile. In desperation, she finally decided to walk out. With her income tax form, along with lunch and some dry socks in her packsack, she set out for Moose Lake, her feet shod only in tennis shoes. She figured these would create the least problem if she fell through somewhere. Taking care to walk on the most solid ice, she swung to shore whenever she encountered open water around riffles or at spots where currents had worn the ice thin at lake narrows. In spite of being careful, she broke through several times and also had to wade some of the riffles. It took her all day and it was getting cold as she hoofed it to Moose Lake, arriving with her pants frozen from the thighs down and her tennis shoes cased in ice.

Pulling in at Bennett's on Moose Lake, she got her wet clothes off and checked her feet, which were purple, blistered, and swollen. For a couple of days she did little except sit around and soak her feet in hot water, eventually getting the swelling reduced enough that she could squeeze her tennis shoes back on. Then she phoned the Sernaks in Aurora; they drove up and got her, giving her a few more days of recuperation at their house. Her income tax was late that year and she had to pay a penalty—she considered that quite unfair and made it the subject of bitter comment for a long time afterward.

Tennis shoes made an unusual choice of footgear for the North Country, where most woods folk wore leather boots. Dorothy tended to wear whatever she felt was comfortable rather than what was practical. At various times she tried army surplus felt "bunny" boots in extreme cold, but found them clumsy. Also, they were worthless in slush, where they turned soggy. Her basic summer footgear was tennis shoes— soft on her feet, easy to care for, and cheap. If a pair wore out, she simply threw them away and bought another. In the winter, she often wore four-buckle overshoes over her sneakers, an arrangement that seemed to work and became sort of a trademark. That type of footgear would probably not have worked with many people, but Dorothy had an unusual amount of energy and excellent blood circulation. She could withstand cold much better than almost anyone else, both physically and mentally.

In November 1969, wilderness guide Harry Lambirth, his dad Claude and brother Bob, guide Andy Hill, Roy Cerny from Mountain Iron, my wife Lil, and I went up to Knife Lake to set up a deer hunting camp. Fall had been unusually warm, and the deer season opened the first part of November. With the temperature in the sixties, we headed up in four square-stern canoes pushed by four three-horse Evinrude motors. When we came across the last portage into Knife, we pulled in at Dorothy's Island and were surprised to find her cabin empty.

"Looks like she's gone out for a visit," Harry Lambirth commented. "Probably gone to Chicago and will try to make it back after freeze-up."

We had no plans to use her cabins, but moved down the shore to set up our tents in a sheltering patch of fir trees on the side of Robbins Island. The weather continued to be incredibly warm; and the first evening, Andy Hill and I trolled up some fish that Claude baked in foil and put together with boiled potatoes and beans. For three days we lived a life of remote luxury, hunting morning and evening, lounging and eating through midday. In three days, we accumulated four deer, from which Claude rendered gourmet dishes of liver-and-onions and sliced boiled heart in gravy on toast.

And then the weather changed abruptly. A howling wind that shook the tents and rattled the flaps like wrapping paper awakened us at 3 A.M. I poked my nose outside and flipped on the flashlight. Already four inches of snow lay on the ground, and the cover was building rapidly. The temperature was plummeting. We had no choice but to get the camp broken down and get moving back to civilization as fast as possible. No doubt a freeze-up would follow on the tail of the storm, and we didn't want to get caught with our canoes frozen in, forcing us to walk out.

By daybreak, we had the tents and sleeping gear packed and the deer stowed in the canoes and were on our way. Going into Knife Portage, with our gloves we shielded our eyes from the driving snow in order to spot the rapids. It was slip-and-slide crossing over, although the snow helped us skid the deer across. Seed and Melon lakes, somewhat sheltered from the gale, gave us a slight respite; then we came out on Carp and paused at the Knife Rapids for a brief rest. In addition to the canoes, motors, and camping gear we had to carry over, we now had five deer, Lil having knocked down one with her .30-30 on the last portage.

We stood eating candy bars on the shore, hunched against

the wind, with snow piling up on our parkas. We saw evidence that the temperature was falling fast: a rim of snow-covered ice was building out from the shorelines in the quieter bays. "It's going to freeze over tonight," Harry warned. "We're getting out just in time."

"We're not out yet," Andy Hill noted. "We've still got another portage and nine miles to Moose Lake."

Just as we prepared to push out into the storm again, we heard the faint drone of an outboard motor in the wind. Puzzled, we cupped our hands to our ears, listening as the sound grew louder. "Who the heck would be out in this?" Claude wondered.

Over the roar of the storm the sound grew more intense, and then out of the swirling flakes appeared a canoe loaded with snow-covered Duluth Packs. Hunched in the stern in her red jacket and no cap, snow piled on her shoulders, was Dorothy Molter, hurrying to get to Knife ahead of the freeze.

"Want a candy bar?" I yelled as her canoe hit the shore.

"No time," she answered. Then noticing our deer, she said: "Hey . . . you guys got lucky . . . what's that . . . four . . . no, five? Pretty good. Hope you didn't shoot Rhonda, my pet deer."

"Nope," Harry affirmed. "We stayed away from your is-land—hunted the main shore. We saw your deer, though, not far from your cabin. Hey, would you like a hand on the portage? With this gang it'll only take a few minutes."

"Oh, no. You better get moving," Dorothy said, sitting down on the bow deck of the canoe and pulling off her overshoes. "The Moose Chain is starting to freeze out from the shore. You've got to get in by dark or you'll never make it tonight."

With that, she threw the overshoes into her canoe, rolled her blue jeans above her knees, grabbed the bow of the canoe, and in her sneakers and bare legs waded up that set of icy rapids.

We stood transfixed until she sloshed around the bend and vanished. "Holy cripes!" Claude said. It was about all any one of us could think to say.

The "Loneliest Woman"

AUTHOR ANDREW HAMILTON started it. In a *Saturday Evening Post* article published in October 1952, Hamilton's story led off with a bold headline announcing: "LONELIEST WOMAN IN AMERICA." And a slightly smaller subhead underneath stated: "Dorothy Molter lives absolutely alone on a remote 10-acre island in the Northeastern Minnesota Wilderness. Even male sportsmen don't dare face the 50-below-zero winters here without any civilized conveniences—the lady likes it that way."

With an eye for detail and an ear for colorful phrases, Hamilton did a superb job of describing the beauty of the Knife Lake area and the lady who could relate so many absorbing tales of life there. Some spectacular color photos by Bill Shrout gave the whole piece the aura of authenticity. And even without any journalistic hype, Dorothy unquestionably did lead a remarkable life.

It made a great story in 1952 and it makes for great reading even today. Of course, it would have made even better reading if it had been true, but such a small detail as truth doesn't take away from the skill of the author. That story not only intrigued the reading public of the United States but started a steady migration of journalists to Knife Lake, each one intent on interviewing and photographing the "loneliest woman in America." As Dorothy once observed wryly, "If I had been the loneliest woman in America, by the time all those writers and TV people came up here, I sure as heck wouldn't have been."

Until the airplane ban took effect in 1953, journalists flew up during the summer in pontoon planes or in the winter in aircraft equipped with aluminum skis. They also came by motor canoe and snowmobile until wilderness law eventually banned all those methods. After that they came by paddle canoe, on skis, and by sled dog until it seemed to Dorothy that every newspaper, magazine, and TV station in the country had a reporter come up at one time or another. Reporters arriving in the summer found the island crawling with Boy Scouts, Girl Scouts, church groups, anglers, and canoe campers. Yet they still somehow managed to write about "the loneliest woman." It continued to make good reading, but to Dorothy and her friends it was all pretty much of a joke.

Anyone who spent much time in the Knife Lake area over the last half century knew "lonely" was far from the case. In the very early years, Dorothy spent only her summers at Isle of Pines, helping Bill Berglund with the resort, sometimes accompanied by Cap and her stepmother. A steady stream of visitors passed through, including dozens of guest anglers at the resort, forest rangers, game wardens, bush pilots, and campers. After Dorothy moved up to stay with Bill in 1934, she spent winters being visited by ice fishermen, trappers, more game wardens, and the occasional hardbitten poacher, sometimes one step ahead of the law.

Dorothy told about one early spring, just after ice-out, when old Gunnar Graves was in the area trying to pick up a little spending money by acquiring a few illegal beaver pelts. A team of game wardens closed in and had him trapped between his camp and his canoe. Graves, like a deer cornered by wolves, slid unobserved into the icy lake and swam across to the island, emerging blue and shaken, two heart beats away from hypothermia. Dorothy got him into the cabin, helped him dry off, and warmed him up with several bowls of hot soup. While the wardens got Graves' equipment and traps, they never did know how he got away. As a principle, Dorothy never condoned poaching, but she had a deep sympathy for the hunted, whether it was running on two feet or four. Graves never forgot and whenever he could do Dorothy a favor or give a hand with chores, he pitched in.

Sometimes in trapping season Dorothy ran the traplines with Bill, but she finally gave that up because she could not abide the overpowering musky smell of the beavers. About the only time she was "alone" in those days came when Berglund went out checking his traps and she had several hours to herself in the cabin—baking, cleaning up, reading, stoking the stove, or putting out food for the host of tiny friends who came to the bird feeder.

After Bill died, the traffic got even heavier. When she hit upon the idea of bottling and selling ice cold root beer, hordes of canoeists, youth groups, families, pairs of anglers, and even lone paddlers made it a point to stop for a cold drink, purchase a candy bar or two, and listen to sage advice on fishing, campsites, and bear problems. On fishing she often said, "It's like anything else—sometimes you get 'em and sometimes you don't—but it isn't because the fish aren't down there." She had little use for thieving bears and kept pretty good track of which campsites were experiencing the most problems with them. "And don't think that just because you're on an island, your camp is safe," she warned. "Heck, they can swim better than you can."

Although she disliked bears, she had even less use for canoeists who made messes at their campsites, cut green trees, peeled birchbark, or left fish entrails on the shore. "Get your firewood back from the shore," she would advise. "When you're on your way back from fishin', pull over to the bank and pick up a canoe load of dead stuff, besides those green trees and branches don't burn worth a darn." And: "You didn't find fish guts when you got to your campsite—well, don't leave any there for the next guy."

Wilderness purists who complained about too many campers would get a quick lecture from Dorothy on getting off their canoe seats and hiking far back into the forest if they wanted to see "real wilderness." She tolerated most people's shortcomings but couldn't stand intolerant people who wanted the world to run their way.

For most visitors, the high point of their trip was usually a visit to Dorothy's, a bottle of root beer, a photo taken standing next to her, and the memory of some sage or hilarious comment.

Not all of the writers who came up got caught in the "loneliest" trap. Dorothy was quick to point out that with six thousand or more visitors signing her guest book each season, probably few women in the world were less lonely. And she was also quick to introduce the numerous members of her family who were at the camp at various times of the year. Her sisters and brothers—Helen, John, Ruth, Bud, and Hazel— were often in camp. And Cap was there off and on all year around as his health permitted. For many years, Isle of Pines was really a family operation, a program that continued into the later decades, when a bevy of growing nephews and nieces began appearing for summer jobs, doing most of the fetch-and-carry chores but also having the times of their lives hiking, canoeing, berry picking, and making root beer with their famous aunt.

Some journalists quickly grasped the real situation on Knife Lake and refrained from that "lonely" issue. Sharon Smickle, reporting for the *Minneapolis Tribune,* wrote a penetrating and truthful piece entitled, "Dorothy Molter/ Remote but not Lonely"; and Thomas C. Cothran did a lengthy article for the

Associated Press laying it out clearly in "Last Canoe Area Resident Isn't Lonely." That her lifestyle was sometimes solitary in no way gave her a feeling of loneliness.

Prior to 1953, when the ban on planes with pontoons and skis went into effect over the BWCA, seldom a week went by in winter without game wardens, trappers, and ice fishermen flying in. All kinds of visitors came and went, some of them pretty crusty old woodsmen. For several winters, visitors to her cabin were surprised to see from a half dozen to a dozen partially filled bottles of whiskey and brandy lined up on the windowsill or along the edge of the table. These, Dorothy assured the curious, were not hers but were "emergency supplies" for the trappers and ice fishermen passing through. On each bottle she had glued a section of notepaper lengthwise over the label, and covering half the container from the bottom to the neck. Each carried the name of the owner, carefully printed out, and a thick black line denoting the level of liquid at the time of the last visit. Dorothy explained that while these hardbitten woodsmen would risk their lives in a blizzard to save even a total stranger, they would brook no meddling with their booze, not even by a close friend. The line assured each bottle owner that no one had sampled his particular supply during his absence.

Sometimes, if Dorothy took a notion she'd like to "chew the rag" with somebody, she snowshoed down to Prairie Portage to visit the Chosas. With the arrival of the snowmobile era, there was often two-way traffic: ice fishermen and trappers coming up to Knife Lake, Dorothy heading out, sometimes just to town, sometimes starting her annual Christmas or New Year's visit to relatives in Chicago, Michigan, or Ohio, visits that took from two weeks to a month.

On the way out and back to the lake, she was a popular guest at Laurel and Gladys Bennett's at Canadian Border Lodge, or perhaps Hollis LaTourell's place, or Larry and Myrt Sernak's in Babbitt. Somewhat of a competition grew up among the people in Ely, Babbitt, and Aurora to see who would have the social prestige of Dorothy's presence.

During the winter of 1967, as she was preparing for her annual Chicago trip, Hollis LaTourell insisted she come down to Babbitt several days early, a commitment she was reluctant to make, since she preferred to take her time packing and usually let the weather decide when she should leave. However, Hollis came up by snowmobile and saw to it that Dorothy came out on a particular Friday, not giving any specific reason. When they got to Babbitt she was startled to find that the city was holding its annual Winter Carnival and she had been chosen guest of honor. At the Friday night basketball game, it fell to Dorothy to crown the queen of the Carnival. The next night, they went to the high school gym for the Saturday dance and Dorothy was astonished to see a huge banner hung over the bandstand: "BABBITT WELCOMES DOROTHY." As a further surprise, during intermission the mayor of Babbitt presented her with an insulated parka, complete with hood, while several hundred citizens, old and young, stood and cheered.

During the 1960s and 1970s, the snowmobile traffic finally got so heavy through the Isle of Pines that Dorothy began looking forward to the time that the ice would be dangerous and no one would show up for a week or two. Clubs, families, quartets, and loners snowmobiled at almost all hours of the day or night. People would simply pull up, stamp up on the porch, and either knock once or yell "Hey Dorothy!" and then barge in. She never had a lock on any door.

"There's so many people stoppin' by here all the time, I can't even take a bath," Dorothy sometimes complained. "I've got to wait until two o'clock in the morning before I can fill the tub with hot water and jump in—and then I've got to keep a towel and my clothes handy in case somebody comes through the front door."

THE "LONELIEST WOMAN"

One Christmas Eve in the 1960s, Julian and Ruth Ann Jones and my wife Lil and I snowmobiled up to Dorothy's with a packsack of cookies, pies, and other bakery goods. Julian had sent word up with ice fishermen several days earlier, letting her know we were coming. Thus we were surprised when we came off the winter portage into Knife Lake, crossed the bay, rode around the point by the island, and saw no lights. We switched off our machines and stood for a moment by the snowdrifted dock, peering at the silent, gray log cabin barely visible under the pines. "Geez, it looks like Dorothy is gone," Julian groaned in disappointment. Ruth Ann had the packsack with the bakery goods hanging over one shoulder and just stood, staring.

Suddenly, a tiny flicker of light shone at the cabin window. Then another. And then a bunch of tiny lights. With a whoop, we plowed through the snow up onto the porch and into the kitchen. Inside, Dorothy had a small Christmas tree anchored to a table by the window, sparkling with dozens of tiny

birthday candles. She had taken bottle caps left over from her root beer operation, removed the cork disk on the underside, pressed the metal caps onto balsam tips, then forced the cork back into place to hold each cap on a branch. Next, she had taken the candles one by one, lighted them, dripped a spot of hot wax on the cap, and anchored each candle in place. She had blown them out and remained quietly inside her cabin in the dark until she heard our machines approach, then struck a match and lit up her tree.

In the warm glow of the candlelight, we shouted Merry Christmases at one another and poured out the contents of our pack. Needing more light, Dorothy lit the gasoline lantern; with that hissing, she sat down to sort out her gifts. While this was going on, we wandered over to the kitchen table, where a Scrabble game was laid out for four people, a game that appeared to be only half finished. No one else seemed to be around, and Ruth Ann inquired, "Somebody playing Scrabble with you?"

"No." Dorothy said glancing up. "I play all four hands myself."

We looked at the rows of letters and the partially finished words. "Well, is that exactly fair?" Ruth Ann asked. "You know all the letters and all the words the other players have."

Dorothy shrugged and gave us one of her semiserious looks. "Yeah? Well, let me tell you—in the last two weeks I haven't been able to beat those other three guys that aren't here."

So much for lonely. And then, of course; there were her friends of the forest. No doubt some city folk couldn't comprehend the bond Dorothy had forged with the wildlife living around her. Some wildlife came to see her, some she went to visit at their places of dwelling. Dorothy was a dedicated walker, something she learned before moving north. She and her sisters thought nothing of hiking ninety blocks to downtown Chicago to see a movie and hiking ninety blocks home afterward. She loved to follow the game trails along Knife Lake's shoreline, observing the beavers, otters, minks, foxes, martens, and fishers. She knew where the eagles, loons, and seagulls nested and she studied the tracks of deer, bears, moose, and wolves, sometimes coming upon one in surprise.

Dorothy's bird feeder was always full of chickadees, nuthatches, grosbeaks, bluejays, and other year-around feathered visitors. During the cold months, downy and hairy woodpeckers clambered up the bark to get at strips of suet anchored to nearby trees. She even gave credit to one of her feathered friends for getting her out of a very difficult situation once when she was alone.

On a warm spring day, just after ice-out, she beached her canoe on the mainland, shouldered a light packsack, and headed for the hills beyond. Intent on finding some new patches of blueberries for picking later, Dorothy was so absorbed in the emerging wildflowers and arrival of new songbirds that she overlooked a shift in the wind. Suddenly, she noticed she no longer cast a shadow. The sun was gone, and what daylight remained was being slowly but surely blotted out by a fog bank drifting in from the southeast. Dorothy fumbled in her pocket for a moment before the realization dawned that she had brought no compass. Now hurrying, she headed back toward where she thought Knife Lake lay, searching for familiar landmarks. Within minutes, mist-shrouded, unfamiliar hills surrounded her and darkness began moving in.

"I was really lost," she admitted. "I had no idea which way was the lakeshore, so I sat down on a log to figure it out. At the very best I was going to spend a cold, wet night in the woods, at least until sunup the next morning when it might clear off and I could get my bearings. Nobody would come looking for me because there wasn't anyone at camp."

And then she heard him, the long, mournful call of Looie the Loon. It sounded faint and far off, but in the misty silence it gave her direct aim toward the lake.

"I took out in that direction, trying to line up trees in order to keep straight, and I stopped every now and then to listen. Looie, bless him, called again and again. It was almost pitch dark when I came out on the lakeshore, but it took only a couple of minutes to locate the canoe, figure out the direction to the island, and paddle home. I was sure glad to get in the cabin, light the lamp, and get a fire started." She paused for a second. "If it hadn't been for Looie, I might still be out there trying to figure out which way it was to the lake."

Coincidence? Probably. But some say the Keeper of the Birds knew Dorothy was lost and had Looie signal her so that she might find her way back. And as some of her friends say, "Who can prove different?"

The Snowmobile Era

THE 1960s ushered the snowmobile era into the North. Home-made, jerry-built snow machines gave way to factory models carrying names like SkiDoo, Arctic Cat, Polaris, Moto Ski, and Scorpion. They were much more dependable, many operating on gas-efficient motorcycle engines. But the conditions in the woods didn't change, and it was still possible to bury the most powerful machine in slush—and they still quit when ice crystals clogged the carburetors. Occasionally, a drive belt exploded in the cold or a worn track came off. Most people traveled in twos or in groups so they could double up and get home in emergencies.

Everyone carried a tool kit, extra spark plugs, and a spray can of ether. In bitter cold, thirty below or colder, common practice was to pull the cover off the air intake, open the choke, and spray ether directly inside. Highly flammable, the ether would usually fire no matter how cold, and once an engine turned over, it could usually be coaxed into running.

Ether could cause problems, however, one being that it could flame back and explode if it was sprayed into the air intake while the snowmobile was running. And the ether spray was infinitely colder than the surrounding air. Once we were up on Knife Lake trout fishing on a subzero day and saw another angler trying to start his engine. He had pulled off his mittens to work on the machine, and when he gave the carburetor a healthy squirt from the ether can, he was holding onto the fuel intake with the free hand. The ether hit the opening but also his hand, which immediately froze hard and white. In the cold, he didn't feel the pain immediately, but it was excruciating when his hand thawed.

A big Sno-Traveler replaced Dorothy's old custom-built machine and almost became Cap's private vehicle. People wishing to buy that first Maser machine made several offers, but Dorothy always turned them down. She used it to haul wood until it finally quit running for good; then it sat quietly under the sheltering pines, like a good work horse put out to pasture after years of service. Snowmobiles sharply increased the winter traffic to Dorothy's. When conditions were good, machines came up every day, sometimes by the bunch on weekends, particularly during the trout season, which opened the first of January. Just as few homes in the North were without a canoe or two in the yard, now there were few that didn't boast of at least one snowmobile. Winton built one of the first snowmobile race tracks in the North, scene of some spectacular early races.

Inevitably, snowmobilers began to organize into clubs with names like "Driftbusters" and "Ely Igloo." Clubs from Grand Marais, Babbitt, Ely, and Winton held "Dorothy Molter Days" on different Sundays during the winter, with sometimes up to a hundred machines converging on Knife Lake. Most of them drove the fourteen miles from Moose Lake, but others came from Winton, through Basswood Lake, close to thirty miles one way. Dorothy, notified well in advance, would have huge cauldrons of soup ready. Sawhorses with planks, set up on the ice near her dock, made serving tables on which gallons of steaming coffee and all manner of other edibles were laid out in potluck fashion. These gala affairs included a lot of laughter and singing, sometimes punctuated with an occasional "pull on the jug."

"The problem with drinking outside in the winter," Dorothy recalled with a laugh, "is that some of those people don't feel it right away. Sometimes they come up to the cabin to get warm and immediately fall sound asleep by the stove—or they go flat on their backs when they walk in the door at home."

One memorable Dorothy Molter Day, Red and Gladys Bennett, Emery Bulinski, Lloyd Nelson, Arvo and Marge Rikkola, and Lil and I went up together. An extra heavy snowfall had blocked off good lake access at Bennett's Canadian Border Lodge, so we trailered our machines to the Moose Lake Public Landing, which the county had thoughtfully plowed. It was one of those crisp North Country winter mornings, with the slanting sun glistening pale yellow on the new snow, shadows from the shoreline trees stretching like dark blue fingers across the lake surface.

Perhaps eighty machines clustered on the lakefront at Dorothy's, with everybody eating and talking all at once and Dorothy ladling out soup along with her usual line of backwoods philosophy. It was "Hi, Dick . . . Hi, Arvo . . . Hello, Jim . . . See you in a couple of weeks when I come down, Gladys . . ." Dorothy never forgot anyone's first name. Last names she had little concern for, but first names were important. "Hey, Joe, did you ever get that big trout weighed? Lloyd, have some more coffee . . ."

As the sun got higher in its winter orbit along the southern rim of trees, the temperature rose and so did the spirits of all present. Inevitably the number of jugs being passed around increased, and when time came to go home, many were in a jovial mood. Some more jovial than others. Until the first

71

machines hit Vera Lake. The warm weather had created an enormous slush pocket on Vera and the fun was gone.

Where we had come across earlier with no trouble, now lay a vast sea of slop a foot deep. The first snowmobiles got buried. As more came behind, we set up a production line, with teams of four or five men and women dragging each machine through the slush to another team of four or five. In this way, we eventually pushed all the machines through to solid pack, although the riders were foot-soaked and covered with ice. By the time the last straggler was accounted for, it was growing dark; we pushed down on the throttles, heading for Moose Lake.

Lloyd Nelson, with true Scandinavian gallantry, had been leading a number of "toasts" to various persons, living and dead, during the day, and had been tirelessly working in the Vera Lake slush. Fortunately, he still had most of one jug under the seat of his machine, a supply he occasionally called upon to maintain correct body temperature while wading in the ice water. It didn't seem to have a lot of effect on him other than that we noticed his headlights seemed to stray occasionally from side to side as we came down the Moose Chain and into the public landing.

In the bitter cold, clouds of exhaust floated in the night air from pickup trucks being backed up to a spot where the machines could be run up wooden ramps and into the truck beds or onto two-wheeled trailers. Lloyd had his pickup idling, the ramp in place, as he gunned his snowmobile to put it in the truck bed. Only he missed the ramp completely on the first try. Cursing roundly, he made a circle in the parking lot, gave the machine full throttle, and headed for the ramp again. Unfortunately, Emery Bulinski and Laurel Bennett stood talking in Lloyd's line of approach. Laurel jumped aside, but Emery had his back to Lloyd and didn't see him—nor hear him with all the other engines being gunned in the dark. Lloyd hit Emery square in the back, flattened him in the snow, and ran right over him. However, his aim had been good, and without a pause, he ran his machine up the ramp and banged into the cab of his pickup, where the snowmobile stopped.

Horrified, we rushed to Emery's aid. We pulled him out of the snow and were relieved when he appeared somewhat shaken, but otherwise undamaged. We brushed the snow from Emery and made ready to leave. "What hit me?" our stunned friend inquired.

"Lloyd," we answered.

"I never should have taken my eyes off him," Emery muttered.

In the meantime, Lloyd had left for town without so much as a backward glance. We saw him one day the following week and kidded him about running over Emery. Lloyd swore up and down that he never hit anybody in the parking lot; Laurel corrected him: "No, you just didn't see anybody in the parking lot."

One of the bonuses of the better snowmobiles was the ease they offered in bringing supplies up to Dorothy in the winter, getting Cap in and out, and helping to transport other members of the family who came up on vacation to sample Knife Lake when the snow was drifted five feet deep and the temperatures made trees pop like rifle shots in the night. Snowmobile groups also worked out systems of getting the ice cut and the firewood hauled and split. With a good number of willing hands, all the ice for the summer could be cut and stacked in the ice house in two days.

Sometimes when Dorothy went out for an extended visit, Larry and Myrt Sernak came up from Aurora to "house sit" the cabins. Larry, whose work was seasonal, had midwinter off, which gave him considerable free time. While staying at Dorothy's they went ice fishing, split and stacked wood, and kept an eye on the other cabins.

"Most people who came up and used her cabins in the winter

were very good about leaving money in the jars, but a few would try to sneak by without paying if she wasn't there," Larry remembers. "Once I noticed smoke coming from the Point Cabin and saw some snowmobiles in front. I checked it out and found some guys had moved in, but there was no cash visible. I made sure they put the money in an envelope for Dorothy before they left."

Snowmobiles also made it much easier for Dorothy to keep her bird feeders supplied with seeds and suet. Part of the charm of visiting her cabin in the winter lay in watching the colorful assortment of birds, almost as at an aviary. Sometimes she went outside with food, and the small birds, like her favorite chickadees, landed on her shoulders and head, taking tidbits from her fingers. As a great treat, the local people took their friends "up to Dorothy's" for a visit and let them see a genuine North Woods legend living among her feathered neighbors.

One high point was a visit to Dorothy's old wooden outhouse, which sat on a rise behind the cabin. She kept trails to all the cabins and the outhouse packed for easy walking in the winter and put wood ashes on the "biffy trail" so no one would slip on the way to the toilet. As one started up the hill attention was immediately drawn to a painted sign that simply said: "HURRY!" A little farther along another sign said: "HURRY! HURRY!" And near the top of the hill a more urgent sign read: "HURRY! HURRY! HURRY!" As the door on the outhouse swung open, a fourth sign inside said: "ALL'S WELL THAT END'S WELL."

Among the relatives who came up in the winter were Dorothy's brother Bud, his wife Freda, their son, and grandchildren Norman and Eddie. Dorothy loved all kids, and eleven-year-old Eddie's first trip to the North Woods in the winter entertained her. An ice-cutting crew had been up earlier, and the cutting area had frozen over smoothly, with just a few inches of snow cover. Dorothy got Eddie to shovel off the smooth ice and make himself a skating rink because he had his ice skates along. As she pointed out later, "Eddie spent more time on his seat than on the skates, but he had a good time."

Bud, handy with a soldering iron, had built Dorothy a table out of pop and beer cans. One of her treasured items, it was on display in the yard during the summer time.

Late one December, a quartet of us decided to head for Knife and camp out instead of using a cabin—Kenny Bellows (now a noted bush pilot in Alaska), Emery Bulinski, Lil, and I. Emery said it would be a snap since he had recently acquired a new type of propane heater, which would throw out enough BTUs to keep the tents toasty. We packed all the gear, along with a generous supply of propane cans, and headed for Knife on our snowmobiles. When we swung into Dorothy's, she asked if we had seen any wolves. When we inquired why, she said, "I was going out to get a bucket of water this morning, and as I stepped off the porch I saw fourteen wolves clustered around the water hole in the ice. They were just standing there, looking at me. I didn't know what to do, so I went back inside and thought about taking a shot that way, but I didn't. Some dummy probably cleaned his fish by the hole and the wolves were sniffing the blood."

I went out and got a fresh pail of water, noting the mess of wolf tracks. Dorothy brewed a pot of coffee and then suggested we stay in one of her cabins because it was going to be terribly cold that night.

"No, we've got it made," Emery said. "I've got this new propane heater to keep the tent warm—it's something the manufacturer wants me to try out."

Dorothy was shaking her head as we pulled out for the east end of Robbin's Island where we found a level spot, cleaned off the snow, and pitched the tent. In the bright afternoon sunshine, with the temperature slightly above zero, we kindled a fire and thawed out our prefrozen, foil-wrapped hamburger dinners. Fishing was slow, however, but we thought action might be better in the morning.

Dorothy proved dead right about the weather. That night, the thermometer hit forty below. A steady westerly breeze sent the windchill down perhaps twenty degrees farther. We had our sleeping bags and all the other gear inside the tent, and the propane heater was hissing by the time it was dark. Everything seemed to be going OK until sometime in the night Kenny Bellows woke up and yelled, "Hey! I'm freezing to death!"

The tie on the tent flap was missing, which allowed a scenic view of moonlight on the snow, but also allowed the wind to swish through the opening. On top of that, as the temperature went down, the propane in the little can began to gel and the glow in the heater shrank smaller and smaller until it finally went out. Emery leaned out of his sleeping bag and relit it, but it went out again.

"I'm getting out of here," Bellows said. "You coming?"

Since we were sleeping in most of our clothes, we had only to slip on our boots and parkas and get going. In minutes, we had the machines coughing in the cold and were on our way in the direction of Dorothy's cabin.

It was 2 A.M., and we figured to slide into one of her cabins quietly and let Dorothy know in the morning what had happened. To our surprise, as we came around the point heading into her bay, her lights were on. She stood on the front step waving a flashlight at us.

We rolled to a stop, cut the ignitions on the machines, and stumbled up the steps into her warm kitchen. A pot of coffee bubbled on the stove and the ever-present dishpan was half full of oatmeal cookies. Teeth chattering, we pulled off our mittens and stamped some life into our feet.

"Didn't think you would be up this late," I mumbled.

"Wouldn't have been if I didn't know you guys were up the lake in that tent. When it hit forty below I expected you back any time—you hung in there a lot longer than I thought."

Dorothy insisted that Lil and I stay in her extra bedroom for the night, Emery and Kenny using the Trapper's Cabin. We didn't protest at all. Seconds after Lil and I hit the warm bed, we were asleep. Dorothy already had a fire going in the Trapper's Cabin, so all Emery and Kenny had to do was slide into bed.

The next day was New Year's Eve, and we had decided to get back to Ely before dark to watch the Rose Bowl game on TV. At daybreak, we dimly heard several snowmobiles humming past, ice anglers heading for the Twin Islands or Thunder Point. At 9 A.M. we got stirring to the aroma of pancakes and bacon Dorothy was cooking on the stove.

The thermometer read twenty below and was rising when we left for Robbin's Island. We found our camp intact, and we got the tent rolled up and the sleeping bags packed to go home. Kenny suggested to Emery that he throw the propane heater into the woods. Emery said, no, he had promised to report on it to the manufacturer, but his report would not be particularly glowing.

We motored up to Birch Narrows, where our luck turned good, with the trout coming alive about noon. By three o'clock we had eight silvery trophies on the ice, two of them eight-pounders, and called it quits. We headed back down the lake, stopping at Dorothy's to drop off a trout and pay for the use of the cabin.

Just to show how the weather can change in the Northland, when we arrived at Ely, about sunset, the temperature stood at forty degrees above zero and meltwater ran down the gutters on the streets. An eighty-degree change had taken place in less than twenty-four hours. None of us can remember who won that Rose Bowl game, but we never forgot the night we spent at Knife Lake with that new-fangled propane camp heater in forty-below temperatures, and Dorothy's much-appreciated hospitality.

In order to mark the packed trail on the lakes between Knife and Moose, snowmobilers jammed balsam boughs into the snow every three hundred yards or so. When new snow covered the old track, a rider could follow the established trail by lining up the boughs. There was no underestimating the importance of a packed trail. Because it was hard, cold penetrated through to the solid ice below, keeping slush from forming. But beware if a person wandered off the trail to one side or the other. It usually meant a buried snow machine and lots of work to get it out.

Ice fishermen were forever getting "slushed up" on Knife Lake. Sometimes little or no slush appeared in the morning, but once holes were cut for fishing, the water seeped out, spreading in all directions over the ice but beneath the insulating snow cover. Twin Islands and Thunder Point, both popular trout spots, were always bad for slush. Sometimes, in order to get free, anglers floundered to shore, returned with armloads of balsam branches, and built a platform on top of the snow. Then they pushed, pulled, and lifted their machines out of the slush up onto the platform, where they could clear the track and bogey wheels. Under real bad conditions, they sometimes laid a "bough road" from the slush pocket to solid pack to get out. And sometimes even that didn't work. Numerous times, anglers left the machines on top of boughs and walked to Dorothy's, some four hours distant, stayed in a cabin overnight, and went back the next morning when the slush had become solid ice and they could travel.

Following passage by Congress of the controversial 1978 Boundary Waters Canoe Area Wilderness act, snowmobiles were on the way out. As of January 1984, they could no longer be used in the wilderness. When the time approached, friends felt great concern that Dorothy might be effectively cut off from outside assistance in the winter. True, she had a radio and could call Forest Service Headquarters in an emergency, but no provisions existed for crews to cut her ice, saw her firewood, or bring in supplies. The same law cut off outboard motors, making it difficult to supply Isle of Pines in the summer.

To anyone who would listen, Dorothy berated those environmentalists who backed the snowmobile ban. "Those people don't have any idea what it is like up here in the winter," she said. "They put out propaganda that we are running all over the woods, chasing the deer and whatnot . . . but this is all bunk. We travel on designated routes and over the lakes . . . there is a lot less environmental impact in the winter because the ground is frozen . . . and the snowmobile tracks vanish as soon as spring comes."

She excoriated some of the media people whom she saw come up looking for "damage" and who managed to find a few cans, bottles, or papers, piled them at one ice fishing site, and took photos to show how bad ice anglers were. These media types she considered fakes, and they were definitely not welcome at her cabin.

Summer canoe campers very often sent up clippings from newspapers that ran the tiresome old stories about winter abuse of the wilderness. These infuriated her, and in her annual winter letter, which went to hundreds of her friends, she chided the falseness of these claims and pointed out that the canoe campers had much more impact on the country than the winter users.

Fortunately, Dorothy had some very close friends on the local level in the Forest Service, and they saw to it that Isle of Pines continued to be supplied after the snowmobile and motor ban went into effect.

Dorothy's Angels

DOROTHY HAD THE SPECIAL THING THE FINNS CALL *SISU*, that particular grit and determination to make it no matter what, and the Northland people who knew her recognized sisu when they saw it. When Dorothy decided to stay at Knife Lake after Bill died in 1948, her friends and acquaintances realized that she would need some special help at times to live in that remote area, and people banded together to provide it. It may have been Bernie Carlson who came up with the name "Dorothy's Angels," a term for the network of people who helped her operate after Bill died. A most interesting and varied group made up the Angels, which included some with obvious Christian principles, but a sprinkling of others who were by nature and practice far removed from any religious relationships.

One of the kindest and most dedicated of the Angels was Bernie Carlson himself, who operated Quetico-Superior Outfitters on Moose Lake. At the tender age of five years, Bernie made his first trip to Knife Lake with his dad, Oscar Carlson, a dedicated North Country trout fisherman, like most of the local men with a Scandinavian background. To Oscar, trout provided not merely the raw material for recreation but essential foodstuff, staples that one had a duty to harvest and render into gourmet fare through the family smoke house. Five-year-old Bernie was too young to go out with the men in boats on that first trip to Isle of Pines, but not too young to lend a hand. Bernie had a job standing on the dock with a pole and line, fishing for shiners that the men would use as trout bait. One of Bernie's first memories was of the day he slipped off the dock and fell headfirst into the icy lake water. Luckily, one of the guides saw him tumble in and immediately pulled him out. Bernie remembers Bill Berglund roaring, "Somebody get a life jacket on that kid and make sure he keeps it on!"

On weekend trips from Moose Lake up to Berglund's, the Carlsons packed in whatever Bill had sent word down that he needed, from groceries to hardware. Once they packed in a stove, welded up in Oscar's shop. On return trips they came back with heavy loads of trout—sometimes more than one hundred pounds—allowable under the generous limits of those days. Bernie grew up, went through the Ely school system, guided for outfitters and resorts, completed college, and worked at various construction jobs. Eventually, the wilderness called, and he went into the canoe outfitting business with Fred Handberg, who started Quetico-Superior Outfitters on Moose Lake.

Bernie got to know Dorothy very well; and after Bill died, Bernie acted as her mailman, picking up and sending out her great volume of letters. Dorothy not only entrusted Bernie with her mailbox key but also made him the booking agent for her resort, keeping track of which cabins were rented and who would be going up and coming out. On top of that, he helped handle her money, banking her receipts in Ely and paying bills when required.

"Sometimes I would take a canoe and motor up to Dorothy's for the day, delivering a bag of mail," Bernie recalled. "When I hit the dock, somebody would always yell: 'Hey! The mailman is here!' Dorothy would come running down to get the mailbag."

Often, canoe paddlers who were hanging around looked on with surprise and asked her, "Do you get mail delivery way up here?"

"Dorothy would nod with a straight face and say: 'Sure, the U.S. Post Office delivers the mail everywhere, don't you know?' "

From Dorothy's, Bernie often headed up through Little Knife to Ottertrack Lake and Bennie Ambrose's cabin, delivering any mail Benny might have accumulated in Ely.

He would be back home in Moose Lake by dark.

Mail runs usually meant a couple of extra packsacks of groceries, too. For many years, Dorothy bought most of her groceries at Johnny Buccowich's market in Ely, food packer for most of the outfitters. She came down by canoe, hitched a ride into town from Moose Lake, got her bags and boxes of groceries, then hooked a ride back to Bernie's. Whatever could fit into four or five Duluth Packs, she loaded into the canoe for the trip back to Knife Lake. She left the rest, confident that Bernie or whoever was coming up next would bring it.

Now and again, her gas refrigerator quit, and Dorothy would send word down to Bernie. He notified Chuck Carey, a retired Marine Corps major, who was an expert on appliances. Chuck filled a packsack with his tools and canoed up. Among the other Angels who provided aid, summer and winter, were Red Bennett, Lloyd Nelson, Rabs Camaish, and Arvo Rikkola.

Once this assistance backfired. In fact, it got Dorothy arrested. Someone got the idea that the root beer she sold was not quite as thirst quenching as the real thing, particularly for older canoeists, so a group of Angels packed and portaged several canoe loads of beer up to Isle of Pines. For a brief time, Dorothy did a brisk business in both root beer and real beer, until fate and some "wilderness snitch" stepped in.

Bush pilot Chick Beel, who flew a World War II surplus Waco on floats, tells about flying into Knife Lake one time with Lake

DOROTHY'S ANGELS

County Deputy Sheriff Martin Carlson to investigate a drowning. Two men were missing in a squall; their boat with fishing tackle was found washed up on the shore. Dorothy's island served as headquarters for a crew being brought in to drag the lake, and Martin was sent up to coordinate the effort. As Chick taxied to the dock and tied up, Dorothy came down with a warm greeting. For Chick. She ignored Martin. And continued to ignore him all day. By afternoon, with the dragging process underway, Chick and Martin were preparing to fly out. As they taxied for takeoff, Chick said to Martin, "Seems to me that Dorothy was giving you a cold shoulder—like she didn't want to talk to you."

"Yeah," Martin agreed wearily. "She's mad at me."

"How come?"

"I had to arrest her a couple of weeks ago for bootlegging."

"Bootlegging?" an astounded Chick asked.

"Yeah," Martin continued. "See, she had this beer for sale and some canoe-paddling snitch came through and noticed she didn't have a Lake County beer license. So he filed a complaint with the county and the sheriff sent me up to arrest her."

Chick laughed, but Martin didn't. He didn't have any choice in the matter, but Dorothy blamed him for the arrest. She went back to root beer, but developed somewhat of a feeling of mistrust toward smiling paddlers who came up to her camp "just to look around." And it was a long time before she spoke to Martin again.

A number of snoops appeared over the years, followers of the letter rather than the spirit, who reported her for a variety of assumed rules violations, which included having bottles in the wilderness after the can-and-bottle ban went into effect. These complaints didn't go anywhere when Forest Service personnel pointed out that her root beer bottles were filled and consumed on the premises and were not taken anywhere else in the BWCA. The snoops eventually stopped most of their clamor, but some self-appointed guardians of the wilderness continued pressure to get Dorothy removed, claiming that her cabin, along with that of Benny Ambrose and those of the Chosas, "violated the spirit of the wilderness."

Fishing guide Mike Patterson, John Rosett, Norm Saari, and Bob Engebritson were all Angels. So were members of the snowmobile clubs from Ely, Winton, and Babbitt, and the game wardens. Conservation officer Bob "Jake" Jacobsen, who began patrolling the area between Ely and Gunflint by sled dog and on snowshoes in 1945, frequently visited.

"Jake" twice snowshoed from Moose Lake to the Gunflint Trail and back in thirty-below weather, his only shelter a six-by-eight tarpaulin, perhaps a good test of his Norwegian heritage. In the summer, he cruised the border with a motor and square-stern canoe, often stopping by Dorothy's to have a cup of coffee or just to see how she was doing. Once he arrived to find Dorothy's dad, Cap, in the process of tearing down and over-hauling two outboard motors and the washing machine. In order to keep from losing any parts, Cap had put all the pieces together in a couple of buckets; now, he couldn't for the life of him figure out which belonged to the outboards and which were washing machine parts. Jake, with Dorothy's blessing, put the buckets of parts in his canoe and ferried them back to Laurel Bennett's on Moose Lake, where Laurel had a repairman put the outboards together. There is no record that the washing machine ever became functional again.

Many Angels recognized that Dorothy was poor at keeping track of money. Money simply didn't hold any big interest for her, although she realized that the few dollars she made renting cabins and selling root beer constituted her sole income. At the end of the year, if she had money left over after buying Christmas presents for all her family, she usually bought a new outboard motor, a new canoe, or perhaps a new deer rifle. She kept money in all kinds of containers, including Mason jars, tin cans, buckets, boxes, and paper bags. John Rosett recalls that once Dorothy lost a paper bag containing twenty-five hundred dollars, most of the summer's proceeds. She didn't know if she had misplaced it or if it had been stolen. Finally it turned up, and she sent it down to the Ely bank for deposit. Without any reservations, at one time or another she entrusted all of her friends with money, asking them simply to "bank it" for her.

During one very busy summer, Dorothy had accumulated a large cloth sack full of coins—change collected mainly from the root beer operation. When the sack could hold no more, she asked Jake to take it to the bank in town, but first to stop and have Laurel Bennett look over the coins because Laurel, a collector, would know if some had any extra value. While at Laurel's, Jake cooked up a scheme to have some fun with Dorothy on the next trip up. Jake duly deposited the sack of coins at the Ely bank, but a week later stopped by Dorothy's, walked in with a woeful expression, and stammered apologetically, "Dorothy, you remember the bag of coins you had me take to town?"

"Yeah."

"The ones you wanted put in the bank?"

"Yeah."

"Well . . ." Jake fidgeted uncomfortably. "See, I stopped by the Winton Liquor Store because I was kinda dry and needed a beer . . ."

"Yeah?"

"Well, one thing led to another—you know how guys get when they are drinking. First this guy buys a drink and then that one . . . and then I bought one and the next thing I knew all the coins were gone."

Dorothy glanced at Jake a moment and shrugged. "Well, that's the way it goes sometimes. Say, did I tell you I saw a moose over in Portage Bay last week?"

Chagrined that his little tease didn't work, Jake finally told her that it was all a joke and the coins really were in the bank. It didn't make that much difference to her, one way or the other.

Once on a routine winter patrol along the Boundary Waters, flying Conservation Officer Bob Hodge spotted Dorothy's big snowmobile buried in frozen lake slush where she had gotten stuck several days before. He could tell from the tracks around it that she had tried without success to get it free. Because of poor ice conditions on Knife Lake, Hodge couldn't land; but when he got back to the seaplane base in Ely, he phoned Hollis LaTourell about the problem. On his own snowmobile Hollis immediately headed to Knife Lake, where he found that Dorothy's machine had practically become a part of the frozen lake surface. He went over to Dorothy's cabin, allowed it would take some doing to get the machine free, secured an ax and an ice chisel, and went to work. It took him two days of continuous effort to chop the snowmobile loose, and then it came out as part of a big ice block. Hollis had to chip all the ice loose from the drive belt, gears, and chain. He finally got it started and then returned to Ely. Hollis, a number of people pointed out, was sort of a Super Angel.

Before the federal air ban was enforced in 1953, flights were made regularly to Knife. Pilots like Bill Leithol and Chick Beel flew in with the Sunday Minneapolis newspapers if they were making a trip up that way. Their only fee for this service was a hot cup of coffee and perhaps a slice of Dorothy's fresh blueberry pie. Hoot Hautala flew a variety of items to the resort in his Stinson Voyager, including bedsprings, ladders, boats, canoes, and anything else that could be strapped or tied to the pontoons or skis. Some of Hoot's trips were paid for, and some were free.

Getting the mail up to Dorothy always had priority. In the summer Bernie Carlson took it up, but in the winter whoever was going up at any particular time played mail carrier. Anyone going up on snowshoes, skis, or snowmobile checked in with Bernie first.

Every year, for a period of weeks in the late fall, the lakes

begin to freeze up but the ice is treacherous—not strong enough
to hold up snowmobiles, or sometimes even people on snowshoes. Dorothy always eagerly awaited the first batch of winter
letters, so the Angels made every effort to provide delivery.
And the more hardy or daring local folk had a continuing
competition to see who could be the "first one in" with Dorothy's
winter mail. Bob Jacobsen and Einerd Johnson probably logged
more "first time in" trips than anyone else.

One year, a week after Thanksgiving, a cold snap sent
temperatures skidding below zero for a few nights. The lakes
accumulated a skin of shiny "glaze ice" an inch or more thick.
One evening, Jacobsen called and wanted to know if I was up
to going in with him to deliver the mail in the morning.

"Is the ice OK?" I inquired with considerable doubt.

"Sure—checked it today. Plenty of ice."

"How much is plenty?" I questioned.

"Several inches," Jake said.

We were off the next day as the sun poked over the treeline
like a huge frozen ball of orange sherbet—Jake, Einerd Johnson,
and I. Jake and Einerd both had Bombardier SkiDoos. My
machine was a brand new red-and-black Scorpion with a top
speed of about fifty-five miles per hour, a pretty hot item for
those days. We roared down Moose Lake on the slick ice—
"slippery as spit on a glass doorknob," as the old timers liked
to say. The ice creaked and moaned a few times, which didn't
reassure me a bit. At Moose Narrows, we hugged the shore
because currents had left strips of open water in the channel;
then we took off easterly down the long expanse of Newfound
Lake. We stopped once by Horseshoe Island, where Jake
smacked the ice a few times with his hand ax, broke a hole, and
examined the edge carefully.

"At least two inches of good ice, maybe three," he announced. "Plenty solid."

Two inches did not sound to me like a very heavy layer
between the machines and a swim in thirty feet of ice water, but

on we went. The route up through Ensign and Vera lakes was uneventful, other than that we ran on scant snow and the machines sort of chewed their way over the portages. We came out of Portage Lake and onto Knife to view a somewhat disheartening spectacle: beyond the first islands, the lake lay wide open, sunlight gleaming on the rippling water. Like most deep trout lakes, Knife was always one of the last to freeze and also one of the last to thaw in the spring. The bay to Dorothy's island had a coat of ice, but everything to the east remained unfrozen. In the still air we noted a thin column of smoke rising above the trees from Dorothy's cabin. She would be waiting, we knew, for her mail.

"I think we can make it across," Einerd said, squinting from the open water to the thin ice and back.

"Yeah—it oughta hold us," Jake agreed.

The problem, as I assessed it, was this: if it didn't hold us, that bay was sixty feet deep, and I said so. Einerd gave me a look that would have withered a polar bear, cracked open the throttle on his SkiDoo, and tore off for the island. Like a great sheet of black plastic, the ice swayed and bent beneath the weight of his machine, but it held; and Einerd came out on the far shore holding both hands over his head like a champion boxer. "Let's go!" Jake yelled over the putt-putt of his idling engine.

"I'll be right here when and if you two come back," I said.

Jake thumbed the throttle and zoomed across on Einerd's path. Again the ice bent and creaked, but didn't break. When Jake hit the island, they both disappeared around the point into the bay where Dorothy's cabin stood. I scrounged up some dry birchbark and an armload of dead balsam sticks, kindled a small fire, and sat down. I must have dozed off, because the sound of the returning machines woke me up. Across the bending ice in single file raced Einerd, then Jake, a good interval between them. I had the fire stamped out when they hit the shore.

"OK?" they asked.

"Yeah—get the mail delivered?"

"Sure. Say that ice is plenty strong—you should have come with us. Dorothy had coffee and fresh oatmeal cookies."

"Listen," I said. "You guys were raised in this country and you know what you are doing, but not me. Going across thin ice isn't exactly my package."

They nodded with a mixture of sympathy and, perhaps, contempt, and we headed back home. As we were preparing to part company on Moose Lake, I noticed that on the back of his sled Einerd had a short chunk of wooden two-by-four, wrapped around and around with nylon line.

"What's that for?" I inquired, pointing.

Einerd glanced at the block. "Well, if the SkiDoo goes through the ice, the block will float and the line will unroll as the machine sinks. It will mark the place where the sled went down so we can find it later."

That was the first and last time I ever volunteered to go in with those guys on the first winter mail run.

Some people noticed, from time to time, that Dorothy needed something but wouldn't ask for it. One summer, some anglers observed that her barrel stove was beginning to rust through, and they made her another one. They hauled it up by canoe in October. Others stopped by, noticed the stove was smoking more than usual, took apart the stove pipes, and cleaned them out. If the pipes started to rust badly, which they did regularly, some Angel would bring more sections of pipe up the next trip, or tell somebody coming up that Dorothy needed four or five new pipe sections, and it would get there—and get put in.

The barrel stove had a somewhat lengthy pipe, going up about six feet, then running across the middle of the room, supported by bailing wire hanging from nails in the rafters. Friends forever worried that the pipe would fill up with creosote someday and catch fire, burning down the cabin. On top of that, Dorothy liked to hang wet mittens, socks, underwear, jackets, and pants on nails close to the pipe to dry out. Others expressed concern that one of these items might come in contact with the stove pipe and catch fire, but Dorothy dismissed all those worries with a wave of her hand.

A well-worked-out transportation system existed for Dorothy whenever she came out on a visit. The Bennetts at Canadian Border Lodge saw that she got around Ely for whatever tasks needed doing and then shuttled her down to Babbitt, where the LaTourells or the Sernaks made sure that she got to the Duluth airport for flights to Chicago. A similar arrangement, in reverse, brought her back to Ely on her return. As she got older and more people became concerned with her welfare, friends went by snowmobile to get her, rather than have her ride down alone with a machine that often broke down or got slush-bound. Rides back to Knife Lake from Ely were set up with trappers like Engebritson or Keil, or ice fishermen—whoever happened to have the time. She never made any demands on anyone. Her Angels simply appeared when she needed them.

In the summer, when she came down with her canoe for supplies, canoe outfitters with big towboats—powerful launches with overhead racks to carry canoes—gave her a fast ride back to Carp Falls, as far as a motorboat could go. This chopped off over half of her return trip, but still left several canoe miles and five portages to Knife Lake. Back during the 1960s and early 1970s three of us operated towboats on Moose Lake: Don Beland, Bernie Carlson at Quetico-Superior Outfitters, and me at Canadian Border Outfitters. Dorothy usually needed lifts during the most hectic part of the summer, but one of the three of us could always arrange time to get her up the lake. Bernie and Don did most of the hauling, but sometimes Laurel Bennett called to see if my boat was available.

On one clear, quiet June morning I loaded Dorothy's seventeen-foot square-back Grumman on the rack, stowed her motor, gas can, and four bulging Duluth Packs in the towboat, and headed up the Moose Chain with Dorothy aboard. It took no more than twenty minutes for the seventy-horsepower Mercury to deliver us to Carp Portage, where we unloaded everything on top of a rough rock ledge at the foot of the falls. We had just gotten the last packsack out of the boat and were getting ready to carry across when two husky young paddlers, about twenty-five years old, came over the portage, going the other way. One puffed along under the burden of a seventy-pound canoe; the other had a single packsack. With some loud grunts and groans denoting the severity of their effort, they lay their burdens down and glanced at the gray-haired lady with the four packs, canoe, and motor. Obviously, they didn't know Dorothy, because one of them asked, "Are you going up to Knife Lake?"

"Yep," Dorothy answered.

"Well, we have to go back for another load. Could we give you a hand taking some of your stuff over, mother?"

At the word "mother" Dorothy stiffened visibly, then gave me a mischievous, sidewise glance. As the two young men watched, she swung a sixty-pound Duluth Pack up on her back, then swung another across her chest in front, flipped up the ninety-pound square-stern Grumman, and picked up the outboard motor in her left hand. "If you kids could get those other two packs and the gas can, it would sure help a lot," she said and took off at a fast trot up the portage.

Mouths hanging agape, the young men watched her go. Then they looked back at me, standing in the towboat. I pointed to the two packs and nodded toward the portage. As if jabbed with needles, they jumped, each one grabbing a Duluth Pack, and one the gas can. Off they went after Dorothy. I don't know if they ever found out the identity of that gray-haired "mother" they helped across Carp Portage, but two young men got a quick education in wilderness manners and unknowingly became a pair of one-time Dorothy's Angels.

Bruno, Brunella & Family

"I DON'T KNOW WHAT GETS INTO BRUNO SOMETIMES," Dorothy complained with uncharacteristic vehemence following a raid on her storage building by a pesky bear that made off with thirty cases of Hershey bars. It was an expensive loss, considering that all those candy bars had been trucked from Ely to Moose Lake and then transported by canoe up seven lakes and carried over five portages.

"Seems like Bruno just has to come in and steal whatever he can find—and what he can't steal, he tears up or slobbers all over.

"That goes for Brunella, too," she added as an afterthought. "And for all their worthless kids."

Dorothy had a great reverence for all wildlife, even for the bears if they didn't become too bold or destructive. In her humorous way of naming all wildlife, the bear family came out as Bruno, Brunella, Bruno Jr., and Miss Brunella. However, there was nothing funny about this raid. The bears had broken into the somewhat rickety shed Dorothy had renovated from an old houseboat cabin, a relic of the logging days. The door had been ripped off its hinges, the frame reduced to matchwood, and the wooden walls splintered.

Dorothy and her sister Ruth surveyed the damage with sadness. Slowly, they went about seeing what could be salvaged from the mess, but the old shed obviously was finished as far as offering any sort of shelter for further supplies.

In some years bears caused little trouble, but in others they were just impossible to deal with. In the early days, Bill Berglund had exhibited a measure of tolerance toward the few bears that showed up, but it seemed as though after Dorothy took over the resort, the bear population either increased or grew much more bold. Perhaps a measure of both.

One summer, nine bears invaded the three islands in a bunch. Dorothy's nephews Larry and Lowell spent the large part of one day chasing them from one island to the next until all nine finally took to the water and swam to the mainland. However, some of them swam right back as soon as it got dark.

The black-furred raiders not only caused damage but also robbed us of sleep. One night, just after everyone had settled into bed, a woman and her husband came running up breathlessly from the Point Cabin with the news that a bear had come through the screen door and onto the porch, where he had proceeded to rifle the icebox. Shouts and pan-banging had frightened the bear off, but it had taken one of their clothing packs in the process. Furthermore, they were terrified the bear would return.

Dorothy grabbed the rifle from the corner of the tent and headed for the cabin with Ruth. The bear had vanished; but the icebox lay on its side, the door pulled open, the contents spilled all over the porch. With some effort Ruth and Dorothy got the icebox upright, replaced whatever food hadn't been ruined, then waited for the raider to return. After a couple of fruitless hours of sitting in the dark, they gave up and started back toward the bridge. On the trail, Dorothy spotted something white, bent over, and picked it up. In the beam of the flashlight it turned out to be a very petite pair of white silk panties the bear had apparently pulled out of the packsack he carried off during his raid.

Dorothy inspected the dainty undergarment, held it up against her own ample torso for a comparison, shook her head, and whispered to Ruth: "Looks like that bear scared the lady right out of her pants."

Not only Dorothy's island received attention from Bruno and his kinfolk. Campers all over Knife Lake continually reported theft or damage to food and equipment. Canoeists came in with rueful reports of bears that walked off with food packs, bears that ripped holes in the sides of tents, bears that even climbed trees where packs were supposedly lashed out of reach, chewed off the ropes, and pounced on the packs when they hit the ground. In these instances, Dorothy did her best to replace some of the camper's staples, such as flour, cornmeal, powdered milk, and cooking oil.

Once Larry and Lowell decided it would be fun to camp out at Knife Portage and perhaps pick up a little tip money helping people carry their equipment and canoes across. To avoid bear trouble, they took no food along, instead coming back to the island each day for their meals. Even this didn't work. When they were back having lunch, Bruno, Brunella, and Bruno Jr. ripped into the campsite. Dorothy felt the bears must have been furious over not finding anything to eat, because they shredded the tent and clawed holes in the two sleeping bags. The boys sadly moved back to the island.

"One night, when my nephew Steve was small," Dorothy related, "we were crossing the bridge from the big island when we met a big bear face-on right in the middle. The bridge is only wide enough for one person at a time and I was in front, so I figured it was either him or us. Anyway, I was pretty mad about the whole thing, so I ran at the bear, yelling at the top of my lungs and slamming my feet on the floor boards.

"There was a wild clatter of footsteps running down the planks," Dorothy laughed. "Steve went one way and the bear went the other—to see who could get off the bridge first." She thought a moment and added, "I think Steve won the race."

But that was more than enough for Dorothy. She marched to the tent, got the old .30-30 out of the corner, loaded it up, and headed back to the main island. Unfortunately for the bear, he stuck around a trifle too long. Dorothy dispatched him with one well-placed shot between the eyes.

"I was curious as to what that bandit had been into, so I cut him open and examined his stomach," Dorothy said. "Along with some other junk he had swallowed a green plastic bag, a small tin can, some wadded-up paper, some small plastic food pouches, some tin foil, and a piece of rope. There doesn't seem to be any limit to what a bear will swipe. I wouldn't be a bit surprised sometime to see a bear coming out of the woods wearing sunglasses and a pink bikini."

One incident, however, Dorothy did not laugh about. It was the only time she was truly frightened.

"I was coming back from Ely with a load of stuff—four packsacks, one of them full of candy bars," she remembered. "I had intended to head back early, before dark, and told Steve to meet me at the upper portage about nine o'clock. Only with one thing and another, I didn't get away from Moose Lake until it was getting toward sunset."

Dorothy thought for a moment and continued. "See, in the morning coming down, I met some campers who said they encountered a big bear at Carp Portage. It simply shuffled up and grabbed one of their food packs that was sitting on the ground. They yelled, but it just growled and carried the pack back into the brush. They were too frightened to pursue it. I wanted to get past that portage before dark, but instead I got there right at dark."

In the gathering gloom, as she cut back the throttle on the outboard, the thunder of the falls filled the night. Like a ghostly gray finger, a dead cedar poked up from the shallows where the current swirled out into Birch Lake. Other than the rush of water, she heard nothing. The trail which led back from the shore lay invisible, shadowed by the towering pines and thick underbrush.

"You know, the real portage is to the left," Dorothy continued. "It runs along the edge of the falls. What most people think is the portage is the old overflow channel where the water comes down during high water in the spring. In fact, we sometimes waded right up that current, dragging the canoes."

The overflow portage, as veteran canoeists know, is a very rocky, rough trail, although amply wide and fairly straight. Dorothy took this trail, a Duluth Pack on her back and another on the front, the canoe on her shoulders, and the outboard motor in her left hand. Walking carefully, feeling her way with her feet, she negotiated the trail and came out on the Carp Lake end without incident. "Halfway there," she thought as she slid the canoe from her shoulders into the shallow water. She loaded the two packsacks just behind the bow seat and clamped the outboard to the transom.

On the return trip, still walking carefully, she was tuned to any rustle, any sound of breaking twigs, but none came. With the last two packs, she retraced her steps and came out on Carp Lake once more with a big sigh of relief. "If I was going to have trouble with Bruno, I was sure it would be on the portage," she said.

"I loaded the last two packs just behind the center thwart and was ready to push off when something didn't seem just right. I waded up to the front and looked down. One of the first Duluth Packs I had carried across was missing. And then I got a powerful whiff of bear smell.

"Now what? Without a flashlight, I didn't know what to do. I was fearful that the stolen packsack was the one with all the candy bars."

With considerable caution, she took a few steps back up the

portage, stopped, and listened. Other than the boom of the falls, she heard no sound in the pitch black night.

"I took a few more steps, up to where the path forked from the overflow toward the falls, and spotted something on the ground. It looked like a candy bar wrapper. As I bent over to pick it up, I got a powerful whiff of bear smell—and I got that feeling I wasn't alone. Looking up, I made out the form of a huge bear silhouetted against the sky, just an arm's length away. He was standing on his back legs, his eyes and teeth gleaming in the dark. If I had taken one more step, I would have run right into him."

Instinctively, Dorothy froze in her tracks. The bear let out a low, menacing growl.

"That just about scared the wits out of me, all alone in the dark with that huge bear," Dorothy said. "I wanted to run for the canoe, but I knew that running was the worst thing I could do."

After a long pause to gather her composure, and with Bruno still growling, Dorothy edged one foot carefully backward, then the other, feeling with her toes to avoid tripping on the rocks. "He kept growling, but he didn't move," she said. "I kept easing slowly backward until I felt the cold metal side of the canoe against my leg. Then I reached down, slid the canoe off the rocks and farther into the water, dropped onto the seat, grabbed the paddle, and gave the canoe a couple of healthy shoves toward the open lake."

At this point, she let out what she felt were her most fearsome war whoops, hoping they would be most insulting to Bruno. Then, somewhat shakily, she cranked up the outboard and finally felt some measure of relief as it sputtered, then roared into motion. Still shaken, she chose not to carry across the remaining portages, but waded up the rapids instead, pulling the loaded canoe by a rope. It was nearly midnight when she finally came out at Knife Portage to the welcome signal of flashlights held by Steve, his cousin, a visiting friend, Bob

Cotton, and Bob's sons. In the yellow gleam of the lights, Dorothy ran the canoe bow up onto the gravel, stepped out, and related her harrowing experience. As they unloaded the packs, they quickly discovered that the missing Duluth Pack was indeed the one loaded with candy bars.

"I never heard Dorothy swear in all the years I was up there," Steve recalled. "But this was one time when I think she was close to it."

The canoe and motor were left on the downstream side of the portage for the boys to use in the morning. They had volunteered to make a quick trip back to Carp Falls in search of the missing pack—or whatever might remain of it—as soon as daylight came. No one got much sleep in the few remaining hours of darkness, and at the first hint of dawn, Steve and his cousin were off for the portage.

Carp Lake lay slick and still as the bow of the Grumman curved into the channel where the water picks up speed just before it tumbles in a cauldron of froth into Birch Lake. In the morning mist, a pair of redheaded mergansers splashed across the surface, wings flailing. Finally airborne, they cut low up the lakeshore on short, staccato wingbeats. With the motor silent, the canoe coasted to the rocky shore. Steve and his cousin climbed out and studied the deserted portage. The overall insistent thunder of the falls made it difficult to tell if anything was moving in the brush as the boys started cautiously down the path. Just a short way ahead, they spotted the stolen packsack. One side had sustained a large rip, but otherwise it looked fairly intact. Oddly enough, at least half of the contents appeared to be still inside. Glancing to the right and left, with considerable apprehension, Steve grabbed up the pack. They dashed back to the canoe, pushed off, and headed straight for Knife Lake. When they arrived back at camp, Dorothy came down to the landing as Steve shut off the motor and tossed the pack onto the dock.

"Doesn't look too bad," she mused, fingering the rip. She

unbuckled the straps and dumped out the contents. Only one carton of candy bars was missing. None of the others had been touched. Somewhat mystified, Dorothy checked the boxes and then exclaimed, "Hey—Bruno only took the carton of Butterfingers! The Hershey bars, Baby Ruths, and Snickers are all intact! Can you imagine that? He only ate the Butterfingers. What a very particular thief!"

Then she looked down the lake toward the portage: "You know, he ate an awful lot of sugar. Do you suppose we should go down there with a hypodermic needle and give him a shot of insulin?" Dorothy said laughing. "Or maybe we ought to go down and give him a shot with the rifle."

Of course they did neither. But the incident of the very particular thief became one of Dorothy's favorite stories.

Winter Letters

"HI, EVERYBODY: Remember me? I'm the pileated woodpecker who lives in a tall white pine right outside Dorothy's window and I'm the fellow who pounds on the trees every morning at the crack of dawn and wakes up the neighborhood for miles around."

So starts the 1959 "Christmas Letter" from the Isle of Pines, one of a series of letters Dorothy wrote and had printed for mailing to hundreds of guests and friends each year. As in this one, she often had one of her bird friends ghostwrite it. The 1959 letter continues:

"Dorothy calls me Mr. Pilly, but the books have a lot of names for me like Lord God Woodpecker . . . Great Black Woodpecker . . . the people I wake up at dawn have special names for me that you don't see in the bird books, or even in the dictionary . . .

"I have lots of fun chiseling holes in Dorothy's nice big pine trees. She doesn't like the way I go around pecking big holes in her trees but I'm such a handsome fellow, and I am a lot of company for her in the winter . . . summer, too, so she has to overlook my bad habits."

Then Mr. Pilly goes on to describe his life in the woods and his wife and family. Dorothy had a keen eye for detail and could paint word pictures of the huge red, black, and white bird in a way that brought it to life for her readers hundreds of miles away. In addition to a library of bird books, Dorothy had binoculars, which she used to study each new bird she came across. Over the years, she became expert at identifying feathered dwellers on Knife Lake—not only by sight but also by their calls—and gained insights into the lives of specific birds, which made her letters eminently readable.

Mr. Pilly's letter continues: "I have my troubles in this world, too. One spring, when I was first married, after my wife and I had our home all nice and cozy, we went on a short honeymoon. When we came back, to our dismay, a pair of flickers had invaded our home and took complete possession. I was pretty mad at them and I scolded and threatened and did everything I could think of to chase them away, but nothing doing. Then Mrs. Flicker said she was expecting the stork pretty quick—so couldn't turn her out then. After that, we became friends and I'd watch her nest while she was out. When the kids were born, she invited me over to see them. My gosh! Such homely things! I wouldn't have the nerve to show them off to the neighbors."

Readers laughed, but the stories brought back fond memories of Knife Lake and the lady who lived there. Those word pictures became family treasures for many, some of their fondest recollections of Christmas time.

In 1961, the letter starts off:

"This is me . . . Louie the Loon. I arrived at Knife Lake last April while the lake was still nearly all covered with ice. I had lots of fun at that time, sticking my head up through the holes in the ice to watch Dorothy chopping wood or carrying water for cleaning the cabins.

"Between campers and us birds, it gets pretty noisy. But I guess I'm the loudest one all right, and I fear sometimes the campers would like to tie my mouth shut for awhile. You can hear me all day long, and all night, too."

Dorothy went on to describe Minnesota's official state bird in detail, although it was all related as coming from Louie. Over the years, Dorothy had picked up dead loons, and she could describe not only the color but the feel of the feathers. She noted how their huge feet were set far back so they could dive more than one hundred feet deep, how their nests were built, the appearance of the eggs, and how they hatched. Dorothy's keen eyes were enhanced by a small camera, with which she took hundreds of photos that filled several albums.

When tragedy struck her summer tent camp in 1955, she reported it directly, without any bird intermediary. "I was lingering over my umpteenth cup of coffee," she wrote. "I did have some trouble with my kerosene stove when I cooked breakfast, but it seemed to be doing all right again, so I put a tea kettle of water on to heat for the dishes. Suddenly, the flame shot up and I turned the burner off right away and tried to smother the fire . . . the flame no sooner hit the tent ceiling when the fire spread like lightning. I used all the water I had in the tent and ran to carry gallons and gallons more.

"I called dad as quick as I could get my breath . . . and soon both of us became fighting firemen in the woods, but not very successful ones . . . the tent went up that quick. So, although we lost the tent and most of its contents, we managed to keep the fire from spreading over the island. I can replace a lot of things I had in the tent, but I can't replace the trees or my island . . . so I thank the Lord that the damage was no worse."

Some three thousand of her photos went up in that fire, along with all the money collected from the spring resort business. Dorothy saved her movie camera and binoculars, although the cases to both were gone.

"I had a few fingers burned dragging the mattresses to the lake," she noted, "but I couldn't let that bother me. My brother (Bud) and his family came up the day after and he helped me to rebuild the tent and make new furniture."

The December 1960 winter letter begins: "Merry Christmas Everybody: It's that time of the year again. This is me, the white wing crossbill. Some people think I am a freak of nature because my bill is crossed. I'm not a freak. My bill is crossed for a purpose."

Through the "voice" of the bird itself, Dorothy went on to explain how the bird uses that bill to extract seeds from pine cones.

In December 1962, hundreds of Dorothy's friends received a letter in the mail with the salutation: "GREETINGS OF THE SEASON! I'm Hairy Woodpecker, and my friend here is Mr. Downy. We both look alike, but I am much bigger. His measurement from tip of bill to tip of tail are six to seven inches. My measurements are from eight to ten inches. We are both year around residents . . ."

Hairy relates that he is shy and loves the woods, but Downy likes both the woods and towns and also likes people. Then Hairy invites the reader to move up closer while he describes his plumage and his friend's in detail. Dorothy wrote in a way that would entertain the avid bird watcher yet still provide enough general notes so the occasional wilderness visitor could identify these two woodpeckers on future canoe trips.

Hairy went on to say: "Well, let's join Dorothy in a coffee clutch (her term). You folks have your coffee and snacks and we will go to work on this bacon rind and peanut butter before the lumberjack, whiskey jack, or camp robber (Canada jay) gets here. I'll keep right on talking and give you the lowdown on Knife Lake activities this past year. Umm, yum-yum! This bacon rind is good. How's the coffee?"

WINTER LETTERS

In this interesting and informal way, Dorothy then chronicled life at Knife Lake from the previous winter on through spring, summer, and fall, up to the current Christmas season. She signed off saying: "And thank you, everyone, for being so good to Dorothy and us birds. Cherrio! from Dorothy and Hairy Woodpecker."

Each letter consisted of four or more pages, painting word pictures for readers in cities across the nation. From their memories of Isle of Pines in the summer, they could follow Dorothy's description of the same area in the winter with the lake covered by ice, a thick blanket of snow on the cabin roof, and gleaming icicles hanging from the eaves. In imagination, they could see this hardy woman of the forest bent over her table by lantern light, carefully pecking out her letter on an old, battered typewriter. As Dorothy's message came through to them, it drew them to the North, let them sit inside the cabin while snow swirled at forty below zero outside, savoring the smell of coffee brewing, observing the pattern of frost crystals on the windows.

One of the winter letters was supposedly written from a warmer climate. It leads off: "Hm . . . it's such a beautiful, warm, sunshiny day here—just like a day in June."

"Here," we discover, is somewhere in Central America. We learn that Dorothy's correspondent is a ruby-throated hummingbird named "Hummy," who is keeping in touch with the chickadees at Knife Lake. They, in turn, relate that the lakes are all frozen over and the cabin windows sheathed with frost. Hummy tells his life history in the first person, then relates what Dorothy did during the year—about her friends coming up by snowmobile with supplies and the mail. We discover that Dorothy took a chance on visiting Ely over deteriorating snow and ice in April with Bob Engebritson, who took the snowmobile across the portages while Dorothy walked. On the portage to Vera Lake: "All went well until she was nearly across the swamp, then missed her step and went flying through the air, making a twopoint landing—that is smack on her face with some kind of fancy twist that left one leg and the camera arm fairly high in the air and the other forequarter and hindquarter somewhere in the mud and tangle under the ice. The water was only a foot or so deep, but when you go in sideways, you come out dripping a little more than when you just get one foot in."

Painfully cold? Undoubtedly, but to Dorothy it was all a big joke. Hummy ends the letter by saying: "Dorothy and all our bird friends would like to wish you all the health and happiness possible in the new year and loads of luck, good friends, and good cheer." Many readers who received this warm message straight from Dorothy's heart found they had damp eyes.

The 1965 winter letter informs us that "all birdland went into an uproar this fall, and feathers and fur flew all over the place for awhile. It all started when Bruno and Brunella Bear said they were going to write this year's letter for Dorothy. None of the birds would stand for it. In the first place, I don't think Dorothy likes bears well enough to let them write. All they think about is stealing. In the second place, they would fall asleep on the job and sleep the rest of the winter. Why, they were both so sleepy when they made the announcement that they yawned and stretched after every word . . . we were sure glad to get rid of them."

Immersed in the battle between bears and birds, the reader moves on to find the correspondent is Billy Blue Jay, who describes himself as ". . . very bold and noisy, and at times I even steal bird's eggs . . . but not near so much as people blame me for . . . I am a very beautiful bird, which is a good thing, because it makes people forget some of the bad things I do."

A year-around resident at Isle of Pines, the jay relates a page of tightly written narration concerning its nesting habits and lists some of its relatives, including the California jay, Florida jay, and Canada jay. "I am also related to the crows, ravens and magpies," says Bill Blue Jay. "Ugh! I suppose that is where I got my bad habits. (But) I'm sure if people knew about me and my relatives better they would forgive us our faults."

As the blue jay chronicles the events of the year, some of Dorothy's humor bubbles out. Her sister Helen and nephews Larry and Lowell and niece Helen visited her for much of the summer. We learn that Dorothy and her niece spent considerable time paddling the shorelines and hiking the wooded hills, especially in search of blueberries. "Everybody at Dorothy's likes blueberry pies, so she had a standing golden rule: 'no pickie, no eatie'—so everyone took turns picking."

About Dorothy's cousin Gert, who came up in July, Jay says: "Gert is afraid of water and . . . took the boat journey even though she was shaking in her boots so bad she rocked the boat and blamed it on the waves. Dorothy made ice cream one day to settle Gerty's nerves, but it soon turned out that everyone on the island had nerves, so there was no ice cream left . . . "

The letter points out that an unusual amount of rain fell all summer and fall, offering the tip that canoeists should be careful in the rapids. Note is taken of two paddlers in October who tried running the rapids and went in "with a splash that made 'Old Faithful' look faithless."

Billy Blue Jay explains: "Dorothy always wades the canoe down rather than riding it because she thinks it's safer that way, and she has more control over the canoe. Dorothy prefers doing the rapids by herself. If she thinks she can't make it, then she will carry the portage. After all, she is not trying to catch a bus, so she has plenty of time."

Tips on camping methods that worked better than others sprinkled each winter letter, yet they were never preachy. Sometimes a hilarious example illustrated the advice, showing Dorothy making the wrong move and getting wet or cold, or having some painful experience. She could be sharply critical of paddlers exercising poor judgment, but always with a forgiving touch. However, woe unto those who misused the wilderness! She told her readers: "In the summer, the Forest Service has men going around cleaning up the dirty campsites. This gives the impression that the campers leave their campsites spotless. Oh man! Is that ever a false alarm! Now, don't get me wrong, for there are just loads of good campers . . . It's just too bad though that we have to suffer for the offenders. It's a shame the way (some) campers are cutting down trees . . . just to watch a tree fall . . . (and) in the summer so many canoeists strike a lucky day and keep right on fishing beyond their limits, drag the fish around on a stringer all day, take pictures and then throw them back in the water . . . after the fish are so far gone they can't live."

Dorothy was a proponent of catch-and-release of gamefish long before the sportsmen's organizations and outdoor magazines picked up the phrase.

The 1967–68 letter, which was printed in booklet form and is treasured even by people who never met her, is probably Dorothy's finest. It begins: "Greetings from my aerie on Knife Lake where there are only two seasons in a year—that's 10 months of winter and two months of cold weather.

"This is really a switch for me. I'm used to sitting high in a tree, seemingly on top of the world, and now, here I am acting as Dorothy's secretary. Now we are together again and we'll see what we can do. She has her pot of coffee handy and I have my rotten fish just outside.

"I am Baldy the Bald Eagle, or the American Eagle if you prefer it that way. A few call me the White-headed Eagle. I live on Knife Lake and am a permanent resident here, and I have relatives living all over the woods. But we respect one another and build our homes three to five miles apart and farther. That way we don't interfere with each other's feeding grounds and are less likely to run out of food.

"My nest is called a aerie, eyrie, eyrey whichever way you prefer to spell it, it's all the same. It is built high in a tree, in the crotch, sometimes eighty feet high or more. It is cup-shaped in the center and lined with small twigs, vines, grass, pine roots, and other small roots. It is bulky, heavy and strong and may be five to eight feet in diameter and seven feet or more deep. Often, odd things abound in the nest like a fish plug, light bulb, table cloth, papers, etc. Us eagles mate for life and only if our mates die do we take on another.

"Us bald eagles mostly dine on dead fish washed up ashore, or occasionally we catch a fish fresh, but we prefer dead ones."

With her keen eyes, Dorothy recorded the constant battles between eagles and ospreys, the latter being excellent fishers and the eagles diving on them to steal their catch.

"Away back some umpty-ump years ago we were battle emblems of the Romans," Baldy continued. "They figured we stood for strength and courage and they decorated banners and staffs and other fighting equipment with our resemblances. Some early American Indians caught us and made pets for their children."

Moving to the news of the year, Baldy tells about a tornadolike storm that ripped through Knife Lake in the spring and took down many of the huge pines on the island. This electrical storm "struck a little storage building near Dorothy's tent and splintered it up some, but there was no serious damage. Two of her friends from California were here at the time and one man fell down for no apparent reason and he felt pretty foolish sitting there on the ground. When the storm was over, Dorothy traced the lightning grooves . . . to the place where the man was standing, so she thinks that's what knocked him down. Fortunately he wasn't hurt."

That spring, big storms and a lot of rain led to a deluge roaring down the Knife Lake basin, which tore out the remains of the old logging dam at Carp Falls and demolished the big dam at Prairie Portage. Almost overnight, Basswood Lake went up five feet, and the lakes above, particularly Moose and Newfound, dropped a similar amount. The Forest Service put a temporary dam by an island at the end of Moose Lake and then installed a sort of railroad with iron rails and a small cart, on which boats could be pushed over the island from Moose into Newfound. Construction started almost immediately on the dam at Prairie Portage. By the end of summer, Dorothy noted, it was holding water and lake levels were getting back to normal.

Baldy pointed out that Dorothy still hiked to town at times and on one hike found three sets of deer antlers and one very nice set of moose antlers. "She tied the moose antlers together . . . put the deer antlers in her packsack, set the pack on the moose antlers, which served as a sled and pulled them across the (frozen) lake . . ."

Dorothy hung up the antlers on display, and when tourists would ask, she would say, "Yep, those are the antlers Baldy wrote about."

Dorothy apologized in the 1967–68 letter for not writing in 1965 and 1966. The reason, she wrote, was that the federal government had condemned her property under the Wilderness Act and threatened to evict her. After considerable furor, they finally granted her tenancy to 1975, and she was very depressed over this, but was now trying to pull herself together.

Baldy's letter concluded: "Very best of wishes to everyone and may you have a healthy and prosperous year. When you come up next summer, look for me . . . high in the top of the trees . . . But don't get a stiff neck looking up . . . may God bless you and keep you. Sincerely, your friends Baldy Eagle and Dorothy."

Dorothy was sixty-two when the Bald Eagle letter arrived in homes across America. Hearts went out to this valiant woman, who was battling a seemingly mindless bureaucracy intent on taking her home on Knife Lake. Few dry eyes were left among families who read this winter letter. And there are few dry eyes today among the old-timers who reread the booklet sent out by Baldy and Dorothy in 1969.

Neighbors,
Wise and Otherwise

IN THE KNIFE LAKE AREA, Dorothy had a number of friends and acquaintances—two-footed, four-footed, and feathered—with whom she was on first-name terms. Her best-known neighbor, a World War I veteran named Benny Ambrose, lived on nearby Ottertrack Lake, to the east.

Originally from Iowa, in 1917 Benny was drafted into the U.S. Army, where he served with a young Ojibwa boy from Grand Marais. Benny heard stories of fish-filled drinking-water lakes, emerald forests, and limitless numbers of valuable fur-bearers just waiting to be trapped. He also heard whispered stories of gold perhaps located in Northeastern Minnesota.

So when Benny was discharged, he made a beeline for the Gunflint Trail, intending to support himself by trapping while seeking the mother lode.

He traveled all over the Superior-Quetico area, becoming one of the most self-sufficient woodsmen in the North. He was on

117

excellent terms with Ojibwa people from Grand Portage to Atikokan, Ontario. They, in turn, respected him and showed him some of the best trapping and fishing areas. He regularly took his furs up to Mine Centre, Ontario, for sale, and sometimes did some gold prospecting up that way. Benny took ore samples from hundreds of sites, but the only real gold he ever found was in the pockets of wealthy sportsmen who came north to canoe, camp, and catch fish under the guidance of this legendary outdoorsman.

Benny homesteaded and settled on the south shore of Ottertrack Lake because he found its clean, fish-filled waters to his liking. In 1940, he married a pretty college graduate who was filled with the romance of the great North Woods; however, after two daughters were born, she gave Benny an ultimatum: build a real house or she would leave. Benny put it off. She left with the two girls. Benny never quite recovered from that, although his two daughters came up from time to time in later years to visit their famous backwoods father.

After Dorothy moved to Knife Lake in the 1930s, Benny occasionally came down to visit, and she went up to his place by canoe at times to share a cup of coffee. The productive vegetable and flower gardens he tended near his cabin astonished her. He grew most of his foodstuffs other than the meat he shot and the berries he picked in the forest. His flower garden created an eye-catching burst of color on the lakeshore.

"Where'd you find a place with dirt up in this rocky country?" Dorothy inquired.

"Didn't find it—brought it in," Benny laughed. He said he hauled countless packsacks full of dirt by canoe, some from Minnesota farmland farther south, some from the organic muck around beaver ponds. He took a couple of canoeloads of dirt down to Dorothy to get her started, and showed her how to dig black dirt from the beaver areas.

Benny told Dorothy about one time he had some trouble with the Forest Service over storing canoes and boats in the federal

Benny Ambrose

wilderness. A new regulation had come out prohibiting such use, and Benny was warned that his stored watercraft would be confiscated and he would be arrested.

"He liked to laugh about that one," Dorothy confided. "Benny wrote a letter to one of his fishing clients, a U.S. Supreme Court justice. All of a sudden, the watercraft storage regulation no longer applied to Benny."

Sometimes when members of her family came up, Dorothy scheduled a one-day canoe trip to Ottertrack Lake so her nieces and nephews could visit with one of North America's most self-sufficient woodsmen. Benny died in his canvas-covered summer cookshack in 1982, at age eighty-four. A memorial service took place a few days later on the site, and dozens of people from Grand Marais, Gunflint, and Ely—Dorothy included—attended. Shan Walshe, the Ontario Parks naturalist, wrote a moving epitaph to Benny, which was published in the Atikokan newspaper.

NEIGHBORS, WISE AND OTHERWISE

Another of Dorothy's neighbors is still alive at age eighty, and still takes canoe trips to that same lake each summer. His real name is Pete Cosme, but he has been known since the 1940s as Knife Lake Pete. He is always one of the first into Knife on ice-out, and usually one of the last coming down in the fall. For years, he worked as a guide for Bernie Carlson's Quetico-Superior Outfitters on Moose Lake. In the late fall he stayed in a small trailer on the canoe base property until the end of the deer season, when he headed back to his home in Chicago.

Raised a block from Comiskey Park, playing field of the Chicago White Sox, Pete grew up as sort of a street-wise kid who learned to hustle a dollar bill wherever he could. Naturally gifted as a bowler, he haunted the alleys, knocking over pins for money and doing quite well at it. With his bowling money, he regularly bet on horses, increasing his stake by judicious handicapping. This allowed him to live in a comfortable but modest style and provided the wherewithal for summer adventures on Knife Lake. He went up there every year from 1939 to 1991, except from 1942 to 1945, when he served as a soldier in World War II.

When Pete came down to visit Dorothy, which was quite often, he brought some of his famous campsite bakery goods, including pies, cakes, doughnuts, and bread. The only problem anyone ever had with Pete was getting him to understand things. Pete had a hearing problem, and until he got a hearing aid in later years, he had to be practically yelled at. And, like many people with uncorrected hearing impairments, he tended to yell loudly when he talked.

Bud Dickson, the co-owner of Canada North Outfitters in Ontario, started out many years ago as a young portage crew member with the Ontario Department of Lands and Forests. On his first trip out, his supervisor gave him an order: "There's somebody camping on the Canadian side of Knife Lake with no permit. Go down and get him out of there or arrest him."

With considerable determination, Bud and his paddle part-

120

ner journeyed through the park and down to Knife, cruising the shoreline until they located Pete's camp. As their canoe hit the shore, Pete emerged from the woods with a big grin and yelled, "Hey! Come on up to my tent! I just got done baking a couple of blueberry pies and I've got hot coffee on the stove!"

"We went up to his tent," Bud recalled, "all set to run him off. Well, he stuffed us full of fresh blueberry pie and coffee, and when we went to leave, loaded us down with doughnuts and fresh-baked bread. Every time I started to bring up the illegal camping, he would cup a hand to his ear and yell, 'What?' We finally just walked down to the shore, got in the canoe and paddled away."

"What are we going to tell the supervisor?" Bud's partner asked with apprehension.

Bud shrugged. "We'll tell him we never found the guy."

However, Pete eventually moved his camp to an island on the United States side and stayed away from Quetico Park. Like Dorothy, he helped uncountable numbers of canoe paddlers in trouble, people who dumped their canoes and lost some of their gear or food. And like Dorothy, Pete's watercraft preference was a Grumman seventeen-foot square-stern canoe pushed by a three-horsepower outboard. He had been going into the wilderness for almost forty years when Congress passed a law banning the use of outboard motors. Pete, sixty-seven at the time, considered this an excellent example of government foolishness as well as an affront to senior citizens, so he simply ignored it. A day came when Pete was heading up to his camp with a canoeload of packsacks and met a group of paddle purists on a portage. Pete got his canoe and gear across, loaded up, mounted the motor on the stern, and was just getting ready to jerk the starter cord when one of the purists hollered, "Hey! You can't do that!"

"Do what?" Pete yelled back, cocking his best ear toward the purist.

"Go with a motor! This is a paddle-only lake."

Pete glanced at the group and solemnly announced, "No, that's only for the members of the Sierra Club—and I'm not a member." With that, he started the motor and headed up the lake.

When Pete came down in the fall to stay in the trailer at Bernie's, he spent most of his waking hours baking bread, doughnuts, pies, and cakes, and he even made up pizzas, ready for the oven. With a Duluth Pack on his back, he regularly walked the whole shore of Moose Lake, dropping off bakery goods anywhere he could find somebody home. With cold weather, he headed back to Chicago, the bowling alleys, the bookies, and the ponies.

Dorothy's four-legged neighbors were all year-around residents. Her beloved cocker spaniel, Peg, died in 1955 at age eleven, leaving Dorothy heart-broken. "Peg went everywhere I went," Dorothy related, tearfully. "She was my shadow. If I got out of her sight for five minutes she came sniffing around looking for me. If I had to go to town and couldn't take her along, she actually got sick until I came back." Dorothy never got another dog, saying she couldn't stand losing it.

But she never ran out of pets. She had pet minks at different times—Mickey and Stinky. Dorothy found Mickey in a trap with his leg broken, took him to her cabin, and nursed him until his leg grew better. Mickey got used to Dorothy, so that he would eat fish out of her hand, but would never climb up in her lap or let her touch him. When the tourist season was over, she turned him loose so he could get ready for winter. He hung around for more than a year and then finally vanished.

Stinky was different. Two of Dorothy's nephews found him swimming in the lake and hauled him out in a landing net. He was about two weeks old, very small, bedraggled, and half-drowned. They wrapped him in a jacket for warmth and brought him to Dorothy's tent.

"Gee, he was a little tyke," Dorothy said, "no bigger than a chipmunk." She used a medicine dropper to feed him warm milk, but soon he learned to feed himself—first bread and milk (no crust, please!), then minnows, liver, hamburger, and larger fish, both cooked and raw.

Dorothy kept Stinky in a large metal mesh cage complete with a section of hollow tree, a swing, a rubber ball, tiny bells on a string, and a sleeping box. In the center of the cage stood a large, square pan full of water for him to drink or swim in. Whenever someone had leftover minnows from fishing, they brought them in, dumped them in the pan, and watched Stinky stalk the minnows for dinner.

Dorothy often took Stinky out of his cage, and he would climb up on her shoulders and sometimes down inside the front of her shirt. "Tourists used to get startled," she noted, "when they were sitting with me drinking coffee and all of a sudden the mink would poke his head out between the first and second buttons of my shirt."

As Stinky got older, he also got a stronger scent. Usually, he smelled very little at all, but like other members of the genus *Mustelidae*—which includes the skunks—when he was frightened, he could emit a powerful odor. On top of that, his claws got longer. Dorothy acquired several scars around her middle in memory of a few races he held inside her shirt. He also nipped her fingers, but only playfully, and never drew blood.

When Dorothy moved from the tent to the cabin in the winter, she took Stinky along. She put paper down inside the cabin and began to slowly "housebreak" him. However, once he got the run of the cabin, he became almost uncontrollable.

"He got into the cupboard where I kept all my magazines," Dorothy complained, "and pushed them all out onto the floor. Then he jumped on the table and made it impossible for me to write letters. He would try to jerk the pencil out of my hand and if that failed, he would climb up on my shoulders and nip at my nose."

For a while, Dorothy let Stinky stay in the cabin at night, but she couldn't get much sleep because he continually prowled about, knocking over vases so he could play in the water running across the tablecloth. Finally, she decided he had to be freed, particularly with winter coming on. She put his cage outside with the door open and kept an eye on him. "At first he didn't seem to care for his freedom. He'd get out of his cage, circle it a few times, and climb right back in again. But after a few days, he wandered to the lakeshore, then went all around the island."

At last, totally wild, Stinky made his winter home in the woodpile near the cabin and Dorothy never saw him again, although she saw his tracks in the snow all winter and into the spring.

That same winter, Dorothy had a weasel come to visit—and then take up residence. It first came in during the night to tear and tug at the suet she kept in a small wire basket fastened to a tree. Then she put some suet on the porch, and when he got that, she put some near the cabin door. The weasel found he could flatten out and squeeze under the door, visiting Dorothy and feasting on suet indoors all winter long. He also cleaned up all the mice around the area.

For three years, Dorothy had a pet deer that wandered around her island. Named "Wanda," it could be fed by hand and was popular with the many canoeists who paddled in for bottled root beer. When hunters came up during deer season, Dorothy warned them to watch out for Wanda, and they never shot her. Dorothy was not against hunting, and when young, she shot her own deer. As she grew older, she stopped hunting and relied on her friends to drop off a hindquarter of venison or two. But she always worried about Wanda. However, it wasn't a hunter that did in her pet. One day, as she headed for town on snowshoes, she came upon the remains of Wanda on the ice where a wolf pack had pulled her down.

"I think Wanda just got too trusting," Dorothy said later, shaking her head sadly.

Dennis the Menace was a pet for just one summer, for which Dorothy was thankful. Dennis was a tiny black bear cub brought in by campers who found him abandoned and squalling on a portage. Dennis quickly fit into Dorothy's household and became a popular member of the family. Tourists loved getting their photos taken with the friendly cub; but as he grew bigger, he could never understand that there was a difference between a piece of candy someone handed him and a whole carton of candy bars stored in the tent. Someone had to continually watch Dennis to shoo him away from supplies. Still, Dorothy didn't have the heart to dispatch him with her old .30-30 Winchester. When fall arrived, Dennis became less active, eventually moving into the woods and denning up. The following spring, much to Dorothy's relief, he left and never returned.

One pet gave Dorothy some real trouble, but only in an indirect way. In the spring of 1960, she adopted a tiny orphaned red squirrel that she found near the cabin and named him Alvin. Using the medicine dropper, she fed him milk until he could take solid food. She kept Alvin indoors, and he even went to bed with her, sleeping under the pillow. The squirrel was always getting into things; and one day as it ducked behind the stove, Dorothy bent over to pick it up and rammed the handle of the water dipper into her eye.

"I knew it was a real problem and required a doctor," Dorothy related. "So the first thing the next morning, I headed for town by canoe with my little nephew Ralph. The eye was not only troublesome, it affected the other eye and I could barely see at all. We stayed a couple of days in town, until I could make things out a little bit, then we headed back. Luckily, we met Ray Grunert, guiding some fishermen from Canadian Border Lodge, and Ray gave us a hand getting the canoe and gear across the first portage. From there we stumbled and fumbled our way back to Knife Lake."

Dorothy's eye got better and Alvin got a train ride to Chicago with Dorothy's niece, Betty, when she left to go home at the end of the summer. The caged squirrel rode in the baggage car, where he was a favorite with the train crew. Back in Chicago, Betty took Alvin to school, where his antics entertained the kids and the teachers. The neighbors came over often to watch him. When the family took him to a restaurant, the guests and waitresses were amused to see him eat ice cream out of a dish.

Alvin had the run of the house much of the time and, since he was housebroken, used a litter box in the kitchen. One morning, when the family got up, they found Alvin dead. He had developed a habit of chewing on the furniture, and they guessed he swallowed some varnish that did him in.

Over the years, Dorothy had a pet snowshoe rabbit, a couple of beavers that she fed at the shoreline, two mink, a weasel, a screech owl, a crow, a bear, and a white-throated sparrow. But her favorite, the one that provided the most laughs, was Vera the crow.

Its full name was Vera Tick, so named because it was found on the Vera Lake portage by a couple of young campers at the height of the tick season. Too young to fly, Vera had fallen out of a tree and suffered a broken wing. The boys brought her to Dorothy, who determined that the crow was perhaps ten weeks old. As with Stinky, Dorothy fed Vera with the medicine dropper, but more often. Vera liked to complain loudly when hungry, which was almost all the time. When Dorothy's sister Ruth came up with her kids for the summer, the kids took over most of the feeding chores. One day, when they were feeding the crow with the medicine dropper, it suddenly lunged forward and swallowed dropper and all. The boys were terrified and came in yelling. Dorothy sized up the situation, took a pair of tweezers, and began probing down the bird's throat.

"I wedged her mouth open, but I couldn't see any sign of the medicine dropper," Dorothy recalled. "I felt around with the tweezers and found something soft but couldn't tell if it was part of Vera's anatomy or not. I didn't want to pull anything out until I knew for sure what I had hold of. I felt around some more and found the glass . . . and the rubber bulb . . . and finally got it out. It did something to Vera's throat, though, because she couldn't make a sound for two weeks."

Everybody was glad when the crow could finally feed itself, although even when full grown she would complain loudly for people to feed her.

"One day I heard a robin scolding from its nest in the tree by the tent and I went out to look. Here was Vera perched on a branch by the nest, head tilted back and mouth open like the baby robins, begging for the mama robin to feed her."

"As Vera grew older, she developed into a kleptomaniac," Dorothy confided. "She'd carry off clothespins, bottle caps, papers, dishrags, nails, fishing lures or anything else that struck her fancy. One day, we couldn't find Ruth's false teeth. We thought at first that Dad had hidden them for a trick, so we didn't say anything, waiting to see what would develop.

"I was hanging out the clothes, trying to keep Vera from swiping the clothespins, when she suddenly appeared with something strange in her bill. I moved closer and made out Ruth's teeth. When I yelled, Ruth came out and got them away from Vera but not without a pretty good argument. I wish I had gotten that on my movie camera. Vera was so mad she flew over to the flower garden and picked off every single blossom."

Because of the damaged wing, Vera spent a long time learning to fly. First, she just took a few short glides around the tent. One day, Ruth and Dorothy were on another island picking blueberries when Vera flew over to watch—her first "long flight." From that point on, she flew all over the islands. She also began spending time with other crows, screaming at them in crow language.

Vera loved to land on people's shoulders and ride around the camp. She found out that if she went down and sat on a boat seat, she could often get a motorboat ride from someone. As the summer waned, Dorothy began to worry what would happen to Vera when winter came. This dilemma was solved in a somewhat tragic fashion: nephews Roger and Bobby came in one morning with the remains of a dead crow. It was Vera Tick, her life terminated by an unfriendly hawk. With due ceremony and a few tears, the beloved clown of the camp, Vera Tick, was buried next to the rose bushes, where she would be remembered every summer when the flowers bloomed.

Cap

Stitched through the Dorothy Molter saga runs the strong, durable thread of her dad, Cap. Sometimes contrary and cantankerous, sometimes generous and funloving, Cap set standards of honesty and self-discipline to which he expected family adherence. He dealt almost all of his working life with thieves who preyed on the railroads, men who made a career of breaking into freight cars to steal their contents. His strict interpretation of right and wrong, based in a strong belief in the Ten Commandments, bred a contempt for the criminals who rightly feared him. He gave complete loyalty to his employer, the Baltimore and Ohio Railroad, and his sense of duty led to frequent commendations and advancements, even during the depression years when many men felt thankful just to be holding down a job.

That sense of personal duty carried over into his family life, ensuring that his wife and youngsters always had a comfortable home, enough to eat, and good schools to attend. In turn, he demanded and received loyalty and obedience from his family.

CAP

"We all had our jobs at home," Dorothy recalled. "We never took time out for ourselves until the work was completed . . . and this included Saturdays when we wanted so badly to go downtown or take in a movie. Always, the work at home came first."

And Cap loved to fish. Fishing seemed to be one activity in which Cap could lose all the bitterness and rancor he felt toward the dishonest and sometimes vicious elements of American society, those whom he dealt with daily as a policeman. Out on the lake, with a fish rod in his hands, sunshine warming his old plaid shirt, he became absorbed in the panorama of endless sky, rippling water, and tree-shaded shoreline. To him it was a reaffirmation that God's creation had beauty, order, and purpose. Furthermore, he loved to eat fish. When he began spending his summers with his daughter at Knife Lake, he saw to it that fillets of walleyes, lake trout, or pike appeared regularly on the menu. In the 1950s, following the stocking of smallmouth bass in the Knife Lake area by members of the Ely-Winton Rod & Gun Club, that game fish species multiplied and rapidly spread along the border waters. Great schools of broad-bodied, jut-jawed bass provided an additional attraction to an already thriving sport fishery.

"They're not quite as good eating as walleyes or lake trout," Cap observed about these finny newcomers, "but they sure fight like the devil."

In the summer, Cap regularly left the dock right after breakfast in a resort boat, returning before supper with a full stringer of fish. There was scarcely a reef, bay, or weedbed he didn't know intimately. As a source of information on where the fish were biting, and on what, he added a valuable asset to the Isle of Pines resort operation. And if guests had trouble catching fish, Cap could sometimes be persuaded to take them out or, at the very least, mark some of the best spots on their fishing maps. When he caught more fish than were needed for immediate table use, he gladly shared with less fortunate anglers.

CAP

Cap was always tinkering with outboard motors, helping with the little store, or hauling firewood. When guests were on the island, he could be a colorful storyteller. One of his favorites involved a highly visible cross erected in a cairn of stones on Robbin's Island, just northeast of Isle of Pines. When visitors asked about the cross, Cap would launch into the story.

"Terrible thing happened there in 1928," Cap began. "Couple of guys up here trout fishin' right after ice-out in the spring swamped their canoe in the ice water but grabbed hold of it, one at each end. They started to swim for shore, pullin' the canoe." Cap paused as though watching the scene unfold, and then continued, "Guy in front kept looking back to see if his buddy was OK, saw him slip off, so he swam back and grabbed his partner's jacket as he was goin' under. Got him back holdin' onto the canoe and asked him if he was all right. Said he was, so the guy in front swam back to the bow and started pullin' the canoe for shore."

At this point, Cap took off his glasses, blew his breath on them, and carefully wiped them off with his handkerchief while the tourists waited in suspense.

"Well, sir, the canoe was only about a hundred feet from the bank, almost to where they could reach bottom with their feet and walk out. The guy swimming in front looked back again and his partner was missing. Just vanished.

"Tired as he was, he swam back and dove under but couldn't see a thing. He was nearly a goner himself, but he made it to the shore, crawled up on the land and collapsed. Luckily, it was a fairly warm day and he had on wool clothing, which probably saved his life because he finally woke up and managed to get a fire started. Well, he yelled for help, but there wasn't any help around right away so he put more wood on the fire and then sat down and made a cross by lashing two poles together with fish line. Then he stuck it up on a pile of rocks.

"Never did find that other feller," Cap observed. "They sent up a crew and they dragged all over that bay but they never got him." Cap scratched the beard stubble on his chin and squinted across the lake. "He's down there yet . . . someplace," he added, ominously.

The cries by the man stranded on Robbin's Island had eventually been heard by Bill Berglund and guide Charlie Signor, who went up there and found him. They retrieved his canoe, brought him back to camp, and sent word down concerning the drowning. In those days, search and rescue was not as well organized as today, and a crew of game wardens came up to drag for the body, which was never found.

That old wooden cross on Robbin's Island served as a signpost and conversation piece for canoe travelers for years. Eventually, it got badly weathered and started to fall apart. One day, Cap built a new cross, a much sturdier one out of pine boards, painted it blue, and nailed a plaque to the front, inscribed with the man's name and date of the drowning. That cross stayed up for several years, and Cap went up every season to give it a fresh coat of paint.

Then one summer it was gone. Considerable uproar followed, and Cap cursed "those darn souvenir hunters," who he was sure had stolen it. A canoe camper from Duluth, the owner of Marshall Outfitters, happened by at this time, grasped the situation quickly, and volunteered to make a new one. The following fall he came back up with the new cross, which rested on the shore of Robbin's Island for many more seasons, further extending the story of the canoe tragedy.

However, others told a different story. One veteran guide who was involved in the investigation and the dragging effort stated, "There was something very funny about that whole thing. True, the other guy said he was hanging on the canoe at the time, when his partner went down. He claimed he made the cross to mark the spot and when the game wardens came up, he marked the place on the map where the cross was and where he said his friend drowned.

"Only the thing was, he refused to go back to Robbin's Island with the game wardens. Now, whatta you think of that? They dragged that whole area back and forth, but they never found the missing guy. And it wasn't very deep in there, either. I was up there when that draggin' was goin' on. Some of us figured there was something awful funny about the whole thing.

"There is still some belief that the missing man may have been murdered on the island and his body hidden or taken out into the middle of the lake and sunk with rocks. Others said the missing guy was runnin' away from something and they just cooked up the story. One thing sure—that guy never did turn up again."

Was it a drowning? A murder? A deception? Several documented drownings happened in Knife Lake while Dorothy lived there, but the bodies were recovered. Although the cross remained up for several decades, the story behind it became one of those unfathomable mysteries interwoven into the history of the North Country . . . and remained a prominent part of Cap's repertoire of stories.

Once Cap discovered he could endure the North Country winters in relative comfort, he became about as much a dedicated snow fan as Dorothy. But, in addition to his chronic diabetes, or because of it, he had poor legs. The snowmobile became his key to winter mobility.

"He loved that machine like a kid with a new toy!" Dorothy exclaimed. "He had a regular route around Knife Lake, picking up and hauling firewood. I would stack up wood on the beach in the early fall, and when he came up he would hitch a sled to the Sno-Traveler and go get it, hauling countless sled loads back to the island over the snowdrifted ice.

"We worked out a system," Dorothy said, "where I would stack up the smaller stuff for Cap to haul home and he would leave the bigger, heavier wood for me to move." Dorothy did this, naturally, with considerable diplomacy, not to belittle her aging father's efforts.

CAP

"Cap was in his glory gettin' firewood, but the trouble was, the machine sometimes got stuck or the engine would quit, and Cap couldn't make his way back.

"Several times Dad went exploring for new places to get wood and got into trouble," Dorothy remembered. "Once I waited until almost dark, then went out looking for him. I followed his snowmobile tracks a way; then they were drifted over and I couldn't tell the fresh tracks from the old ones, so I followed several sets of tracks."

The problem was, they didn't lead to Cap; they led back to the cabin. By then it got too dark to see, so she went inside, secured a flashlight, and started off in a different direction. Still no sign of Cap, so she came back and once more started all over again. She yelled a few times; once she thought she heard somebody a long way off yell back, so she headed for the sound. It was rapidly growing colder, and she was getting panic-stricken that he might be lost in the woods. Whether he could survive all night in the bitter cold was problematical. She yelled again, but the wind drowned out any possible reply.

"I stopped to listen and thought I heard a faint crunching on the snow," Dorothy said. "I listened good, but I couldn't tell if it was a person or an animal. There were wolf tracks all over the snow and I thought it might be a wolf pack. I yelled some more, then heard a voice which certainly wasn't a wolf . . . it was Dad. Not only had the snowmobile stopped, but when he tried to get it going he had somehow set the engine on fire. Because he couldn't walk very well, he was using his snow shovel as a cane."

Dorothy gave Cap the flashlight, then plowed through the snow ahead of him, breaking a trail. It took them an hour and a half to cover the final mile to the cabin. "We were both too bushed to play our usual three games of pinochle before we went to bed that night," she laughed.

Dorothy worried about him continually because of his health. When he felt good, he was spritely and cheerful. When ailing, he became morose and grouchy. In her winter letters through the 1950s, she always signed off with "from Dorothy and Cap," although Cap didn't write any of it. But it made him feel good to be included in the letters going out to hundreds of her friends, all of whom knew and loved Cap. The letters helped forge a stronger bond between father and daughter.

Dorothy always looked for things she thought Cap might be interested in or things she could photograph to show him later. According to the journal she kept daily, one early May she located a mallard hen with a clutch of eleven eggs nested alongside the ice house. She showed this to Cap, who enjoyed watching the eggs hatch out and the chicks swim off with their mother. Dorothy also found a loon's nest that they inspected and filmed. One day, out walking with just her camera, she climbed over a rocky ledge in search of new blueberry patches and was startled to see a nighthawk fluttering along the ground as though injured.

"I could tell by its actions that there was a nest nearby, but try as I would, I couldn't see it," she noted. "Then both nighthawks came up on the ledge, draggin' their wings like they were broken, trying to lead me away; but I just stood there, lookin' around."

Finally, in a little hollow, among some old, dried deer droppings, she spotted a couple of eggs, one of them broken. And then she heard a faint peep.

"I kept looking and made out a tiny ball of fuzz with one shiny black eye peekin' out," Dorothy said. "So I picked up a stem of grass and touched the fuzz. It peeped and moved. It was a baby nighthawk."

Dorothy got some fine photos of the two adult nighthawks doing their crippled wing maneuver and also of the tiny chick. Cap and other members of the family enjoyed these and other films when Dorothy came down on her annual Christmas visit.

Usually Cap went back to Chicago in the fall, sometime in October before freeze-up. Then he came back up in March for the last of winter, and Dorothy met him in town or out at Moose Lake. She parked her snowmobile sometimes at Anderson's Lodge, on Moose, and they left from there. Once when the Andersons were away for the day and Dorothy came in to pick up her dad, Cap took a big stick and wrote in the snow by the Andersons' front door "CAP IS BACK." He not only was proud of his daughter, carving out a life in the rugged wilderness, but was somewhat proud of himself, living out there a good part of the year, too.

In the May 5, 1962, entry in Dorothy's journal, she noted that the ice was breaking up. A few trout fishermen had come through by canoe, picking their way between ice cakes. Hollis LaTourell made it up, bringing in the first mail of spring. Cap was happy to get his mail—letters from the rest of the family he hadn't heard from for a month. It took him two days to read all the mail and answer some of the letters.

"May seventh, Cap got up as usual," Dorothy recalled. "He went down to the dock, getting ready to go fishin'. The trout had been hitting and he had been out the day before with some luck. But after a few minutes he came back to the tent to lay down. Then he got up, coughing.

"Suddenly, he said he couldn't get his breath," Dorothy recalled with a shake of her head, "and before anything could be done, he passed away."

Even though she had been expecting something like this might happen, when it occurred with such suddenness, it came as a shock to Dorothy.

Cap's body was flown to Ely by float plane, then shipped to Chicago on a final train ride. His brothers in the Masonic Lodge prepared an impressive funeral, with all the family and over three hundred friends in attendance. The family requested that any contributions be sent in Cap's name to the Shriners' Hospital for Crippled Children, to the Heart Fund, or to the Ely-Winton Hospital. Still, a lot of flowers arrived at the funeral home, and Dorothy felt they should not be wasted. She and her sister-in-law, Freda, boxed up some of the plants and brought them back to Ely and from there by canoe to Isle of Pines, where they were planted in several of the small plots of dirt Dorothy had sandwiched between the boulders and rock ledges. They became part of the colorful garden that dotted the hillsides above and below the summer tent.

Dorothy not only was depressed when she and Freda got back to the camp but also was apprehensive over what might have taken place during the week she was gone with no one around the premises. She feared that campers might have come in and simply helped themselves to whatever they wanted. Such proved not to be the case. All their canoes, motors, and equipment remained untouched. On the table inside the summer tent she found a number of notes from people who had stopped for a bottle of pop, candy bars, or other supplies, listing whatever they had taken. In a jar next to the notes was more than sixty dollars in cash, lying in plain sight. During that week, with Dorothy gone, each person had simply added his or her amount to that left by the previous customers. Somehow, this example of backwoods honesty seemed to raise Dorothy's spirits a notch. In addition, various members of the family came up to stay until fall, keeping Dorothy company and helping out with the resort. The pain of Cap's death slowly gave way to memories of better times. Cap had become part of the Knife Lake legend.

Ice-cold Root Beer

BAR-RONG! BOO-RONG-RONG-ARRONG! BOR-RONG-RONG-WOR-RONG . . .
WHAROOM!

The piercing sound of the lake freezing over, initially shrill
and high-pitched as the ice first reached from shore to shore,
then deeper and thunderous as the ice got thicker, ushered in
what Dorothy's Ojibwa neighbors called *Gashkadena Geesis* or
the "Ice-forming Moon"—November. To Dorothy, the sound
was nature's orchestral overture to winter and signaled the
time for planning to harvest the companion ingredient to her
ice-cold root beer—the ice.

Cold, clear Knife Lake, as transparent as the sky above it,
produced quality ice each winter. The ice was cut into blocks,
which were then slid across the surface to a snow-slicked
wooden ramp and up into the old wooden icehouse, where
they were carefully stacked and packed with sphagnum moss
and sawdust. This supply carried the resort through the following summer. When Bill Berglund had the resort, he and
Dorothy—and sometimes Joe Chosa—sawed up the cakes by

141

hand, first shoveling the snow off a large section of the lake to get down to clear, hard ice.

There was a science in this. If a cold snap came early, well before heavy snowfall, the lakes froze over solidly. As the temperatures plunged in December, the ice continued to build downward. This produced the best ice, the "blue ice," which was the most durable and melted slowly when put into the resort iceboxes or chipped into shards for drinks. If heavy snowfall came when the ice was thin, however, it pressed the ice down and created slush that froze into "white ice," a product that was full of air and melted and disintegrated rapidly in warm weather. The ice harvesters had to judge when the best time came to gather the good blue ice from the lake surface. Too early, it was not thick enough. Too late, it was apt to be mixed with frozen slush.

During the 1930s and into the 1940s, Berglund's resort and a hundred others from Crane Lake across to Grand Marais all used lake ice put up in the winter. Cutting ice often turned into a festive occasion, with groups of resorters going from one lodge to another, cutting and stacking each other's ice for the following summer. As on grain farms at harvest time, the resort kitchens provided large quantities of steaming food, strong coffee, and perhaps a cauldron of "glug"—a hot Scandinavian drink composed of brandy and wine, flavored with cinnamon and other spices.

As the federal rural electrification program began pushing poles and power into the remote country, accessible resorts were hooked up to the REA lines. Sleek enameled refrigerators began to replace the old wooden iceboxes. But Isle of Pines lay too far in the backwoods to receive electrical lines. For as long as that resort lasted, the ritual of ice cutting and storing occurred regularly each winter.

Prior to President Truman's float plane ban, signed in 1948, pontoon plane operators flew dozens of cases of pop to Knife Lake each summer. These flights continued illegally into 1949 and 1950, but by 1951 arrests were being made. Full bottles could not be flown in and the empties flown out; another means of supplying thirsty anglers had to be devised. Dorothy hit upon the idea of making root beer on the island, bottling and capping it there, and using the winter-cut ice from Knife Lake to provide a tangy, refreshingly cold drink on a hot day.

For over three decades, from 1952 well into the 1980s, Knife Lake became famous as the home of the "Root Beer Lady." Thousands of canoe paddlers visited the Isle of Pines each summer to uncap and consume countless bottles of ice-cold root beer. Many of these visitors never did learn Dorothy's real name—"Root Beer Lady" served perfectly well.

A number of newspaper and magazine articles and several television shows featured the root beer, made and dispensed in the heart of the wilderness. The beverage became a colorful sidelight to North Woods canoe trips; a ritual developed among paddlers, to visit Dorothy and sample her chilled drink. On a sizzling hot July day, veteran canoeists loved to tell unsuspecting newcomers, "We'll stop on the island just ahead and have some ice-cold root beer." The unbelieving neophyte was thoroughly astounded to be served exactly that.

Because of her remote situation and her reputation for living largely off the land, a whole mythology built up around her brewing methods. "Dorothy's root beer is better than anything you can get at any drive-in across the country," many canoeists affirmed. "She's got a formula with her own ingredients . . . something the commercial root beer makers haven't discovered yet. It's just out of this world."

No question, after paddling fourteen miles on a sweltering summer day, that ice-cold drink tasted like elixir from heaven. Conjecture as to just how she made it and what went into it was rife. "I'd give a hundred bucks to know her root beer formula," some thirsty travelers exclaimed. But few could bring themselves to pry into her secret formula—and those who did were astonished by her answer.

ICE-COLD ROOT BEER

Along with the drink, there was the matter of the ice. For urban-bred paddlers, those not old enough to remember the days of the city ice man, to hear how the ice was sawed and put up each winter was an adventure in itself. Their imaginations could picture the harvest of ice cakes from the lake surface, as Dorothy told how they sawed and stacked blocks, sometimes with the thermometer dipping close to forty below zero. And a trip to the icehouse for a peek inside provided a time-warp venture back to the days of their grandparents.

For Dorothy, of course, the harvest of ice held little romance. It was a process as necessary as getting her winter's firewood supply sawed up and stacked, but a lot more difficult. Right after Bill died, in 1948, Dorothy put up most of the ice by herself. She shoveled off a patch of snow, estimating how big an area would need to be cut to fill the ice house. Then she scored the surface with an ax, marking the size of the cakes to be taken out. Next she chipped through, making an opening large enough to get the ice saw blade into the lake. On the side of the shoveled surface toward the ice house, she chipped the ice on a slant, creating a sort of slide to skid the cakes out of the water when they were cut and loosened. When several blocks had been sawed, she pushed them near the edge, gripped them with a tongs, and pulled them from the lake by a rope and pulley. Usually they were about eighteen inches thick, thirty inches in length, and two feet across. From the edge of the lake she skidded them inside the ice house, where she carefully stacked and packed them to a rigid formula, each block fitting snugly against the last.

Ice cutting went best when Dorothy had adequate help. Ice fishermen venturing up to Knife Lake would ask her if it was time to saw. "Don't know if it's thick enough yet," she would answer. A discussion would follow among the anglers as to how thick they thought the surface was when they cut fishing holes. It might be eight inches—or, perhaps, a foot.

"Eighteen inches of good ice'll make it; anything else doesn't store as well," Dorothy pronounced with finality.

The problem was that some winters the ice just got to its cutting "prime" about the time she planned to make her annual visit home to Chicago. This presented a dilemma: should she cut the thinner ice now, or wait until she got back and hope it would be thicker but without the addition of frozen slush?

During the heyday of the snowmobile, groups of parka-clad volunteers came up to help with the winter ice, scheduling their trips to coincide with the best time to cut. These sorties included the Winton, Ely, Babbitt, and Grand Marais snowmobile clubs, plus a lot of individuals who just came on their own when word got around that "it's ice time at Dorothy's." And sometimes her brothers or other relatives came back from Chicago with her to help in the ice block harvest. These were often gala events.

Power saws quickly replaced hand tools. Dick Abrahamson's circle-bladed power saw in the late 1950s was the first, followed by chain saws, which could buck up firewood as well as buzz through the frozen lake surface. The trick was to set the cut so the blade went almost, but not quite, through the ice into the lake. This kept the cutting area free from flying water and resulted in rows of blocks that needed only a hit with a chisel to break them loose and send them floating.

Dorothy allowed any number of cutters to operate, but stacking and storing the ice was done only under her strict supervision. With tongs, she gripped each 150-pound cake as it arrived, flipped it up on edge, and slid it into place with no more effort than if she were flipping around a packsack. Even those outside could hear her voice from within the ice house: "All right . . . get it right up against the moss—get it straight— we gotta get forty more blocks into this first layer."

She saw to it that a thick layer of moss insulation was laid up against the outside walls as each row was stacked.

"Hey—you got a crack there—get some smaller chunks and some snow and fill it in—we don't want any air pockets."

Most of the cakes would fit snugly, but wherever a crack

occurred, they filled it in tight with chipped ice or snow. The top layer was laid horizontally, wide side down, to complete the seal over the upright cakes. In early years, sphagnum moss and bags of sawdust covered the final layer; but in later years, Dorothy acquired sheets of thick blue styrofoam and laid these over the ice. Then sawdust bags made further seal. Any extra cakes were stacked on top of the foam and covered with moss and sawdust, to be the first coming out of the ice house in the spring.

The ice kept surprisingly well in the old wooden building. To get at the blocks in the summer, Dorothy swung open the door, removed the insulation from a small section of the ice, took a cake or two, and then sealed everything back up. The blocks kept cold and firm right into the fall of each year.

In addition to the hazard of bitter cold, sawing ice had an ever-present element of danger. Each winter in those years when ice was regularly cut across the Northland, people rushing about, cutting and sliding out blocks, lost their footing and went into the lake. In most instances, they merely got a dunking in the frigid water; but in several cases, they fell in at an angle and shot out under the ice that had not yet been cut. If they were good swimmers and quick-witted, they looked around when they came up against the frozen surface, tried to see where the most light was coming from, and swam for the hole. But if they didn't come up immediately, their co-workers quickly began probing beneath the ice with poles or boathooks, trying to latch onto their clothes. Sometimes they got out, but the newspapers carried stories of a tragic death or two each year at ice-cutting time in northern Minnesota.

Twice, Dorothy admitted, she slipped and fell into the hole, but being a strong swimmer, she came up immediately. In each case she got out quickly, with nothing more than chattering teeth and limbs turning blue by the time she stumbled into the warmth of her cabin.

Some veteran cutters wore ice cleats—steel claws that

strapped to the sole of the boot and gripped the ice, preventing a slide. The sawyers who worked at the edges of the holes nearly all wore these cleats. They were not as important to workers farther back on solid ice who were roping and skidding the blocks to the ice house.

But it wasn't all work and no play. The ice harvesters took occasional coffee breaks, and Dorothy regularly had a cauldron of venison stew or soup steaming on the top of her barrel stove. Knife Lake's noted trout population caused some lost time, too. The ice-cutting teams frequently found that one or two members had sneaked off to set lines or check ones already set. If the trout were hitting, which happened quite often, some people spent more time baiting hooks, fighting fish, and hauling them through the holes than they did cutting blocks. But somehow the ice always got put up.

During a few winters when Dorothy went to Chicago, a group of her Angels came up on their own and did the whole job. When she got back, the ice house was packed full. On occasions one or more trappers, like Jim Keil, Bob Engebritson, Hollis LaTourell, or Norm Saari, helped her cut and stack the blocks.

Brewing, bottling, and dispensing the root beer constituted an arduous undertaking in itself. When the tourist season was at its height, 150 to 200 visitors arrived daily, each wanting to slug down a drink. Some nights, Dorothy, Cap, sisters, brothers, nephews, nieces, whoever was on hand, worked through to two or three o'clock in the morning, capping beverages for the following day.

Although genuinely tasty and famous, the root beer was only part of the attraction to Isle of Pines. Each visit became a journey into a sort of combination zoo, museum, art gallery, and school of wilderness philosophy. Several hundred mallard ducks padded and quacked about the premises, complaining loudly that they wanted Dorothy to provide another bushel of shelled corn. Song birds continually flew in and out of the feeders; squirrels and chipmunks scurried around or sat up to be hand fed, along with any of the various pet birds and animals Dorothy currently tamed. With each bottle of root beer some advice or philosophy was often advanced.

"How are the bugs this year?" a city-bred paddler inquired.

"The health and welfare of the insect population is no concern of mine," Dorothy shot back.

"How do you find the bears?"

"You don't—they'll find you."

First-time visitors to Dorothy's island, after paddling endless miles of seemingly similar lakeshore, were surprised when they suddenly rounded the point into the bay to be confronted by a large, painted, plywood figure of a uniformed policeman, one gloved hand on his whistle, the other raised palm outward, with the warning: "Stop!"

Above the cop whirled wooden weather vanes. Some were built like birds, with wings that moved in the wind; another was the model of an airplane, with a propeller that spun when there was a breeze. A half dozen large thermometers hung at various points, all of them giving a different temperature reading. Only Dorothy knew which one was right.

Gardens large and small were scattered all over the island wherever soil could be packed between rocks or along granite ledges. In addition to those floral oases, all manner of receptacles—rotting hulls of old wooden boats, boxes, buckets, pots, and baskets—held growing flowers. From every side spilled a profusion of blossoms that created a dazzling, multihued hillside. Dorothy was forever watering, weeding, digging here and there "to let the air in," sometimes transplanting or adding humus. Inside the tent, and sometimes on the pop cooler or an outdoor table, she had vases and Mason jars filled with freshly-cut flowers, replenished on a daily basis. She grew some of her flowers from seed; others, like the roses, were perennials. And some she picked up as boxed seedlings from the Ely Flower and Seed Store in town, packing them by canoe across the lakes and over the portages, fourteen miles to her island.

Although the flowers were incredibly beautiful, probably the most-photographed attraction was the "paddle fence."

"I started the darn thing when I found a broken paddle in the Knife Lake rapids," Dorothy recalled. "I don't know why, but I brought the blade home and stuck it in the ground by the walkway going past my tent. Stuck the next ones there, too."

With an eye for color, she began painting the paddles—red, blue, green, yellow, white, gray, purple, pink, orchid, brown and every shade in between. She sunk some posts in the ground and then nailed peeled fir poles across from the posts to handy trees, creating a frame on which to nail more blades. In the spaces between the blades, she nailed up the broken shafts. Some of the paddles had histories:

"See that blue one there—it's named for Camp Mishawaka— the stern paddler wedged it between two rocks and broke it. That pink one was slapped on the water to make a "beaver sound" and cracked off at the handle. That red one made several trips to Atikokan and back—and would've made some more but somebody dropped a heavy pack on it. Gray, there, met his end when two guys tried to paddle up a rapids instead of portaging around—and Whitey came to grief when two canoe groups were having a water fight."

The list went on. Dorothy knew each paddle and its story. And each one had the name of some group—Boy Scout, Girl Scout, YMCA youth camp, church group—lettered on it. Having a paddle on the paddle fence became a badge of honor, and some groups saved a broken paddle for a week or more, until they got to the island, just to have the prestige of their broken blade on display.

"There just doesn't seem to be any end to the ways people have figured out to break canoe paddles," Dorothy observed.

Through the 1970s and into the 1980s, the root beer business boomed. With the island foot traffic growing more congested, a sign went up: "Please limit your visit to 20 minutes or less." Another one read: "Only two root beers to a customer."

Some summers, Dorothy sold between eleven thousand and twelve thousand bottles of root beer. This also meant that eleven thousand to twelve thousand times, those bottles had been washed, filled, capped in the tent with a hand press, and cooled with ice. The whole family became experts at the root beer process—all except Cap. "Dad never could get the hang of it," Dorothy complained. "His root beer was just awful. He liked to make it, but we tried all kinds of ways to keep him away—he never did get a batch right."

After federal regulations made it illegal for her to sell the root beer, she kept on making it for the next twenty years, "giving it away," but accepting donations from the thirsty and thankful, who put the usual thirty-five cents, or a half dollar, or even folding money into the "donations" jar set on one side of the cooler. Root beer, candy bars, and overnight stays were all paid for by donations. When asked what something cost, Dorothy would shrug and say she couldn't sell anything. But one of her nephews or other family members or old friends passing through would quickly name the minimum price expected. And woe unto anyone who tried to slide through without paying. In such instances, somebody, quite often a total stranger, would sidle up, point to the jar, and firmly order, "Put 'er in there." Forest Service rangers on the trail, well aware of the law, regularly guzzled down cold root beers and put their change in the jar. Quetico Park naturalist Shan Walshe vowed he scheduled his trips in order to swing past Dorothy's on a hot day and would "chug-a-lug four or five bottles—the only thing that would quench your thirst."

Out of the thousands who visited Isle of Pines, inevitably a very few were dishonest. In Dorothy's winter cabin, someone had started a fad one winter by thumb-tacking a dollar bill by the kitchen window. Eventually, dollar bills surrounded the entire window. Then, one summer day, they were gone. A particularly noisy church youth group had been clambering around the island that day, and Dorothy reasoned somebody in the group might be the culprit. She knew the priest who was the group leader and the Ely outfitter where they had come from. The next day, she sent word down to the outfitter's, and when the group came in from their trip, the priest was duly informed. Promising the wrath of God, the good father confronted his charges. The culprit promptly 'fessed up and handed the money over. The next canoe party brought up an envelope with the dollar bills inside. They went back up around the kitchen window.

As the root beer business flourished, year after year, the mythology of its formula and making grew in direct proportion. Naturally, some paddlers were simply overcome with curiosity and ached to discover just what rare ingredients, what roots and herbs Dorothy gathered from the forest to create such an unusually tasty beverage. For those who asked, Dorothy simply and honestly replied, "It's Hires Root Beer Extract. You can get it at any grocery store."

Some were not convinced. They felt she was holding something back. But even those who had their illusions shattered maintained, "Well, it always tasted better up at her place, anyway." Unquestionably, the magic ingredient was the setting—the Isle of Pines and the clear, clean water of Knife Lake.

The Knife Lake War

Oᴜᴛsɪᴅᴇ ᴛʜᴇ ᴄᴀʙɪɴ at Canadian Border Lodge on Moose Lake, the thermometer registered twenty-five below zero. Occasional gusts of January wind kicked up whirling "snow devils" that danced across the drifted surface. But the sun shone and the day promised to warm up somewhat. Furthermore, the winter lake trout season had just opened. That was reason enough for my wife Lil and I to join resort owner Emery Bulinski for a snowmobile run up to Knife Lake for the day.

The winter trail from Newfound Lake was well-packed, and, although furrowed with snow, Ensign Lake provided smooth riding. We negotiated the trail through the tall swamp grass to Vera Lake and then across to Knife Lake. It was midmorning when we pulled up in front of Dorothy's cabin, noting the smoke coming from the stove pipe as we walked up the incline to the porch.

A muffled "C'mon in" answered our knock. We stomped inside the warm, cluttered cabin interior, jerking off our mittens to warm stiff fingers by the barrel stove. Dorothy sat at the kitchen table, but her usual jovial countenance was clouded over. Tears ran down her cheeks.

"What's wrong?" Lil inquired. It took a struggle for Dorothy to speak, but once she started the words tumbled out: "They're throwin' me out . . . takin' my land, my cabin . . . told me I had to get out."

"Who?" Emery and I asked together.

"Government. Two guys came in here yesterday . . . said the land had been condemned and it was now government land . . . and I would have to get out." A fresh avalanche of tears flowed down her weathered cheeks.

"Dorothy," I said quietly. "Nobody's going to throw you out. Let's calm down and talk about this."

It was January 1964, and the federal government was trying to complete land acquisitions within the Boundary Waters Canoe Area. The process harked back to 1930 and the passage of the Shipstead-Newton-Nolan Act, protecting the border lakes from hydroelectric development. That was the same year Dorothy first visited Knife Lake, the visit that set the future course of her life. In the 1930s and later in the 1940s, a number of resort operations arose in what was to officially become the BWCA. In the early days, Forest Service officials believed that establishing resorts in remote areas would provide the public with a wilderness experience in safe, spare, comfortable accommodations, yet keep impact on the resource to a minimum.

Another viewpoint was developing, however. The Izaak Walton League and other conservation groups felt that the Boundary Waters should be for canoe camping exclusively. They began a move to purchase private lands for the purpose of removing cabins and resorts. Impetus for this move escalated during the era of the float planes. Canoe travelers often discovered that after they spent a couple of days paddling and portaging to some remote fishing lake, they confronted groups of wealthy anglers who could afford to fly in, take limits of trout or walleyes in a half day, and fly back out. Float planes also opened up the area to more resort development. To conservation groups, it looked like a race was on to preserve what remained of the wild country.

In 1934, President Franklin Roosevelt appointed the Quetico-Superior Committee, a group of conservationists charged with formulating long-range plans. One of the immediate provisions called for a ban on float planes. At the time, the wilderness had undergone several name changes, from the Forest Wilderness Area to the Primitive Area to the Primitive Roadless Area. Not until 1958 would it finally be called the Boundary Waters Canoe Area.

In 1948, the Thye-Blatnik Act provided $500,000 in federal funds to buy out private lands in the area. This was increased by several million, and in subsequent years the purchases escalated. President Harry Truman issued an executive order banning flights into or over the Boundary Waters under four thousand feet. Up to that point, Dorothy had only hovered in the background, listening to the men talk about the new laws as they sat around the kitchen table in Bill's cabin. But in 1948, Bill died and Dorothy became the sole owner of Isle of Pines. Only she and Benny Ambrose, up on Ottertrack Lake, remained in that remote area. The government, backed by the conservation groups, wanted them out.

In a series of meetings the Forest Service offered to negotiate a settlement with Dorothy. Although she understood what the government wanted to do, she could not understand why.

"What am I doing that endangers the wilderness?" she asked. "I thought all the time I was helping people out—taking out fish hooks, helping the sick, getting assistance for people with busted bones. What am I hurting?"

Forest Service officials had no answer to this other than that "policy" now determined that no interior resorts could be operated, nor could private cabins remain in the wilderness. Reluctantly, Dorothy agreed to sell her land and cabins if she could get enough from the sale to build a new place on either Snowbank or Moose lake, where she also owned property. In its files, the Forest Service lists the first appraisal of her property. It was valued at approximately three thousand dollars.

With over three thousand feet of shoreline involved, on one of the most scenic lakes in the area, Dorothy felt that one dollar a front foot was a pretty shabby price. She wasn't interested.

A report in the Forest Service files from the Kawishiwi District Ranger in 1948 stated: "Because of the physical barriers in reaching this area and with the advent of airplane restrictions, it is doubtful that there would be a sufficient volume of business to operate this resort and trading post profitably." Thus, no value was placed on the resort itself, and there seemed to be a feeling that if let alone, she would go broke. That assessment was certainly in error, because she didn't, although a number of other resorts in the Ely area folded and settled.

Dorothy's presence posed an affront to some conservation groups. By the mid-1950s, other government overtures were made to purchase the islands. The demands got more strident, and Dorothy finally told some of her official visitors that she didn't really enjoy talking to them and would be pleased if they simply stayed away. The government did not accept this rebuke with magnanimity. By 1961, the offer had grown to $19,500, but Dorothy still showed little interest.

"What's it worth to you?" one forest ranger finally asked.

"It's worth $100,000 to me."

Dorothy figured it would take that amount to build a similar small resort on her other property. With no other source of income, she didn't see another choice. The bureaucracy was getting more irritated at this obstinate woman. A formal letter from Superior National Forest Supervisor L. P. Neff stated: "It appears, therefore, that further negotiations will serve no useful purpose to either party. Under the circumstances, we see no alternative than to recommend that condemnation proceedings be initiated to acquire your property."

The government made one more offer. Dorothy could receive $15,500 in cash and remain on the island for life. But she could not operate the resort. "How am I supposed to eat?" Dorothy asked. She ignored the offer as simply absurd.

In 1964, the federal Wilderness Act was passed. With considerable controversy, the Boundary Waters Canoe Area was included. The backers of the new law created a "wilderness definition," which stated that a wilderness is a place where people merely pass through, such as campers in tents, and where no one lives. Dorothy thought this was laughable.

"We've got government scientists up here studyin' this country who say there were people living here for the last eight thousand years," Dorothy noted. "Now some other branch of the government tells us that either those people never lived here or there was no such thing as wilderness in North America until they passed a law this year."

The wheels of the federal judiciary began to grind. In 1964, the condemnation order was completed. The government notified Dorothy that she did not own her land anymore. She would be paid $19,550 but had to get out. Dorothy broke down in tears.

On Ottertrack Lake, to the east, rugged homesteader Benny Ambrose handled the situation a little differently. Benny, the World War I veteran who had carved out a home in the wilderness country, whose friends were trappers and Indians, had become a legend among woodsmen. He looked on the new breed of city-oriented "wilderness" people with contempt, and the federal government as a tyrant. A U.S. Forest Service employee once told me what occurred when uniformed personnel went up to Ottertrack Lake and delivered the condemnation papers to Benny.

"He glanced at them, but didn't read them entirely. He knew what they said because it had been explained to him. He turned the papers over, looked out the window thoughtfully, sighed, then looked back at the men. 'You go tell your boss,' he said evenly, 'that I've got a loaded .30-30 Winchester sitting in the corner of this cabin, and the next person in uniform who steps on my dock is going to get blown into the lake.'

"They got out of there quickly and the district couldn't find anyone who would go back up there," the forester concluded.

That Benny would shoot was without question. And the federal government did not particularly want to send heavily armed marshals up to shoot it out with him—and probably kill him. They would probably lose some people in the process. It was Benny's country and he could last a long time in the woods while they were hunting him down. Also, the public sympathy would go with Benny and the press would have a field day with it. This posed a "no-win" position for the Forest Service, and they knew it.

Now, sitting in Dorothy's cabin, we faced her situation. At this point, few people knew what was happening to her. However, I was then the outdoor editor for the *Chicago Daily News*, and I was up doing some snowmobile stories. Two years later, my wife and I would leave Chicago permanently and move to Moose Lake on the edge of the wilderness; but at the time I was a reporter. Drinking coffee at Dorothy's kitchen table, I took lengthy notes. This, it was obvious, made one heck of a human interest story. It also seemed a gross injustice that would not sit well with the American people once the information was made public.

We didn't do much fishing that day. Frankly, my wife and I and Emery Bulinski were too angry. But we calmed Dorothy down somewhat, and when we left, I told her, "Listen. Don't sign anything. Don't agree to anything. Next time some of your friends come up, tell them what's happening—and tell your lawyer to get on the ball. There is one thing sure: the federal government does not want to get into court with you. A judge or jury would take one look at the power of the federal government trying to kick a nice gray-haired lady out of her home and the government lawyers would get their heads ripped off. Nobody is going to boot you out. Sit tight."

For the first time, she smiled. We shook hands, got on our snowmobiles, and headed back to Moose Lake. I could hardly wait to get back to Chicago and file the story. The *Chicago Daily News* was a leading national newspaper and had a wire service to many other newspapers, similar to the Associated Press service, although considerably smaller. The *Daily News* published the story and it went out on the wire. It was a blockbuster. In two days the story spread all over the United States. Phones began ringing in Washington. Hubert H. Humphrey, U.S. Senator from Minnesota, and U.S. Representative John Blatnik marched over to the Forest Service offices and demanded to know exactly what was going on. Humphrey had been a sponsor of the 1964 Wilderness Act. He was furious.

At the *Daily News* in Chicago, my phone rang. It was L. P. Neff, supervisor of the Superior National Forest. Neff's voice seemed somewhat strained, and he said he felt my story was biased and not exactly accurate. I asked him if he hadn't indeed served Dorothy with eviction papers.

"There's more to it—I would like to talk to you," he said.

"So talk."

"If I fly down to Chicago tomorrow, will you meet me for lunch?"

"Certainly." (No newspaper reporter worth his salt ever turned down a free lunch.)

The following day, at 11:30 A.M., Supervisor Neff met me at the *Daily News* and we went to the nearby Wrigley Building cafeteria. When we had settled at a table, Neff began probing my source of information. He seemed totally surprised to discover that I was familiar with the canoe country, had paddled most of the main trails with my wife, and knew Knife Lake and Dorothy quite well. He seemed like a pleasant, intelligent administrator caught in the gears of the bureaucratic machinery. His current task, it appeared, was damage control.

We sparred over details of the condemnation and he finally asked, "What can I do to get you off my back?"

I had to laugh, although it wasn't polite, because the damage was already done. The government's case had been torpedoed and the ship was sinking in public outrage. Furthermore, I didn't control the situation. But to answer his question, I put it to him evenly, "Let Dorothy alone."

Neff shook his head. "We've got a law to administer. We've tried to reach an agreement with her. She won't budge."

I started to get warm under my collar. "You tried to reach an agreement? You offered her peanuts—your appraisal was lousy. Her place is worth a lot more than $19,000."

Then Neff got a little hot. "The appraisal was fair. We went by the book."

I let out a snort. "Listen. I could put those cabins and that three thousand feet of shoreline up for sale on the Chicago real estate market and get $125,000 for the whole works by tomorrow."

"You can't figure it that way," Neff said.

"That's exactly how you figure it."

Neff looked exasperated. He had made the trip all the way to Chicago and nothing was working. I was sure somebody in Washington, probably the chief of the Forest Service, had told him, "Get down there and get that thing straightened out."

I told him once more, "Let her alone. Hey, somewhere in all those stacks of Forest Service rules and regulations, you can find something that will let Dorothy live out her days up there. You can figure out some kind of an arrangement so that she can stay on Knife Lake, and the government can get the place when she's gone."

Neff shook his head. "We tried that."

"Not really. Not with the kind of money you're talking about. Not with eliminating her livelihood. You wind up in court with that fine, gracious, gray-haired lady and the press is going to rip your head off."

"We don't want to go to court."

"Well, then, do what's right." I felt genuinely sorry for this forester. He no doubt had a distinguished career and was not far from retirement—and then this thing had to explode in his face. It wasn't exactly his fault that the law and the bureaucracy functioned that way. However, as "point man" for the government, he would certainly take the fall if things got worse. We shook hands when he left to catch the flight back to Duluth. But we had no agreement.

In the Ely area, and all across northern Minnesota, the public was up in arms. Even some of the most single-minded environmentalists sent letters to Washington deploring the way the government was going after Dorothy. In the midst of this hooraw, the Forest Service took a bold step. The agency issued a statement that both Dorothy and Benny would be allowed to stay and that negotiations were continuing. The public clamor died down, but the bureaucracy contained some people furious at being thwarted. They weren't done with Dorothy yet.

Subsequent meetings with federal officials resulted in an agreement that Dorothy and Benny could stay in their respective homes until 1975. But the bureaucrats got in the last shot: Dorothy would not be allowed to engage in any commercial activity. She could stay at Isle of Pines but would not be allowed to earn a living. If there had been rage before, it was nothing compared to what Dorothy's friends felt when this came out. The rage simmers in the Ely area to this day. Dorothy, however, was tired of fighting. She signed the agreement. So did Benny. The final payment for Isle of Pines was set at $27,000.

Thus it came about that Dorothy's entire income from that time forward became "voluntary donations." She continued to sell root beer and candy bars and receive rental, occasionally, for two of her cabins, but she never mentioned price. Instead, people put their "donations" in jars and Dorothy survived. The usual few "wilderness snitches," canoe-paddling busybodies, complained to the Forest Service that Dorothy was still selling beverages, but nobody wanted to sign a formal complaint. Nobody dared to take public responsibility for something like that. And the Forest Service did not really want to reopen the controversy. The bad publicity had already cost them a lot more than the $100,000 price Dorothy suggested in the first place. Officialdom and the public assumed that by 1975 both Dorothy and Benny would be either dead or ready to move out.

To everyone's surprise, 1975 arrived and the famous residents of Knife and Ottertrack lakes still lived in their respective cabins and showed no signs of leaving. A new forest supervisor and a new district ranger sought to take a different tack. They appointed Dorothy and Benny as special "volunteers in service," giving them tenancy as long as they wished and assigning them some duties. Dorothy's included: "1. Keep records on the number of people visiting Knife Lake, summer and winter. 2. Assist and provide information to BWCA visitors. 3. Monitor campsite occupancy on the western end of Knife Lake and determine the frequency of overnight use . . ."

Dorothy settled down to a quiet life in the wilderness, but this only endured for three years. In 1978, a new BWCA Wilderness Act came into existence after a bitter fight. Under its provisions, outboard motor use and snowmobiles would be prohibited as of 1984. Up to then, Dorothy, her family members, friends, and Angels, had managed to keep her supplied by motor canoe and snow machine. Dorothy was aging, and friends suggested maybe she should come out to stay before 1984. Family members offered her a home in Chicago.

"I can't stand the cities," Dorothy stated. "I can go to town for supplies and I can go down and visit Chicago for a few weeks, but Knife Lake is my home. I'm going to stay here just as long as I am able."

Meanwhile, a transformation was taking place within the Forest Service itself. The field personnel, the men and women who went out on the canoe trails all summer, cleaning campsites and helping paddlers, had become fond of this gracious, weathered lady who now wore a thatch of snow white hair. Instead of remaining adversaries, the people of the Kawishiwi District and the forest supervisor in Duluth became her protectors. They never missed an opportunity to stop by, have a root beer, and visit—well aware that she was selling root beer when they made their "donation."

Benny died in 1982, but Dorothy went on—slower to be sure, but showing no signs of leaving Isle of Pines. She was now stooped and walked with a shuffle. Her hands had become badly misshapen from arthritis, but her mind remained sharp and her spirit intense.

The forest supervisor, the Kawishiwi ranger, and staff members from the district held a meeting. They formulated an action plan that would provide for flying Dorothy in and out as needed, seeing that she got necessary supplies (including root beer extract to make her contraband beverage), and seeing to it that her wood was cut and ice put up. She could have outboard motor and snowmobile access to Knife Lake for herself and accompanying members of her family or friends, and she could personally use a motor on the lake itself. No one else could use motors.

In addition to supplies being flown in by the Forest Service Beaver, the Voyageur Outward Bound School in Ely volunteered to go up periodically with dogsled teams to cut ice and wood. Communications would be maintained daily on a two-way radio so she could call in her needs, which would go up on the next flight. On the return, trash would be packed out, including some of the items that had accumulated over the past fifty years. She was supplied with a ten-watt USFS radio with a portable antenna and also a rigid one mounted on a tree outside the cabin. She was to call in each day, and the county sheriff's department was on alert in case she called in at night when the Forest Service offices were closed.

Probably no other move the Forest Service undertook after the passage of the Wilderness Act received such universal approval by the people who lived on the edge of the canoe country as did implementing the action plan. The agency, which had once caused her so much trouble, now became Dorothy's staunch friend.

The Final Chapter

"WHAT'RE YOU TWO DOIN' WAY UP HERE?"

Dorothy Molter, bent and weathered like a gnarled cedar that had spent its life on a windswept shoreline, shuffled out of her old canvas-roofed summer tent, flashed her impish grin, and shaded her eyes against the brilliant July sun. It was Dorothy's usual greeting to old friends, and we gave her the usual reply:

"We ran out of root beer."

Dorothy chuckled and aimed a scarred thumb at the old cooler leaning against the tent sidewall. "Root beer's in there—on ice."

While my wife fished two dripping dark brown bottles from the cooler, I scanned the familiar premises, noting the ancient sign still nailed to the plywood tent front: "OUR HOME BREWED ROOT BEER—IT MADE MILWAUKEE JEALOUS." And over to one side, hanging slightly askew, another sign announced: "LIMIT—TWO ROOT BEERS."

THE FINAL CHAPTER

"Had a free day," I explained. "Thought we'd paddle up and make sure the bears didn't getcha."

"Ah, those bears . . ." she waved an arm. "Always tryin' to see if they can make a bigger mess than the campers." She swept a few stray strands of gray back from her forehead. "Lots of people stoppin' by—can't hardly keep up with the danged root beer." The hands that brushed back her hair moved down to lock her arms across her stomach. I noticed with a shock that the fingers were terribly bent from arthritis, worse than I ever remembered. The lines etched in her face were deeper, and those blue eyes, once as piercing as an eagle's, now seemed somehow faded and preoccupied.

A neighbor had given us a lift by motorboat to the Indian Portage into Birch Lake, and from there Lil and I had paddled the eight miles to Knife Lake in about two and one-half hours. It had been Lil's idea to go make the visit.

"Better get up and see Dorothy. Might miss her when she comes out this winter—can't be having too many more years up there."

True, Dorothy would be eighty next May. And talk had gone around Ely that perhaps she would finally recognize the passage of time and would move to town permanently. Others said, "Nope, she's never coming out of there, not while she has anything to say about it."

With just the canoe and a lunch pack, we literally sailed up Birch, rapidly crossed Carp, and negotiated the portages and short paddle stretches to Knife. About the only change since our first trip to Dorothy's, three decades earlier, was the disappearance of the weathered logging dams and sluices at Carp Falls and Knife Portage. Over many seasons, those had rotted, crumbled, and been carried away by water and ice. The portages, worn to bedrock by countless moccasins and boots, probably remained unchanged since the days of the voyageurs and Ojibwa canoemen.

"Can't keep track of time," Dorothy said as we sipped our

drinks. "Seems like we just opened up and here it is the middle of summer already. The ducks are gangin' up to get fed."

"How many ducks are hanging around?" Lil asked.

"Probably a couple hundred," Dorothy shrugged. "Then there's all the other birds . . ." She glanced up into a balsam fir where two chickadees played hide and seek.

The previous fall, 1985, the Forest Service had flown in almost a ton of shelled and cracked corn, hundreds of pounds of sunflower seeds, and other bird food, along with most of the supplies Dorothy would need through the winter and into the spring. Bert Hyde, from the Voyageur Outward Bound on the Kawishiwi River, south of Ely, had hauled in more supplies, including fresh food, all winter long by dogsled.

I took another swig of the sweet, tangy brew. "They tell me there's been a number of writers and TV people coming up this summer."

"Oh, them! Migosh, they won't let a person alone. I told Bernie to tell 'em all to stay home. I don't hardly have enough time to keep this place together without a bunch of people runnin' all over takin' pictures and askin' about a million questions."

"You're big news, Dorothy," I said.

She glanced sharply at me. "News? Say, there were a couple of fellas from some newspaper stopped by here the other day— said they wanted to do a story. I asked them why and they said it would be good publicity for me!" Her eyes lit up with some of the old sparkle. "Publicity? Can you imagine that? With six thousand people coming through here, what in the world would I want with publicity?"

A mischievous look crossed the furrowed face. "I told them if they really wanted to do something, they could help wash out a couple of hundred root beer bottles. You should seen them run for their canoe!"

From somewhere down the lake shore came the clunk of aluminum hitting granite. An elderly, pot-bellied Boy Scout leader in smudged shorts came into view, striding up the path at the head of nine gangly adolescents. More customers.

Lil and I finished off our root beer. "Where's the jar?" Lil inquired, looking for the container designated "DONATIONS."

"Oh, this one's on me," Dorothy grinned.

"No way." I spotted the Mason jar on a dilapidated wood box, fished two singles out of my billfold, and stuffed them in with the rest of the paper money and change. "It gets tougher and tougher to paddle up here every year," I noted. "We're gettin' too darn old."

At that, Dorothy really laughed. "When I was young as you, I used to make that trip alone with a square-stern, seven packs, motor and gas . . . sometimes in the middle of the night."

"You still could," I offered.

"Oh, I don't know about that." Dorothy squinted out toward the sunlight bouncing off the waves. "I think about it sometimes, and I've got legal clearance to do it . . . but the government gets me in and out now." She shrugged and ran a hand over her brow. "Just seems like I'm always so darn tired all the time." She gave a heavy sigh. "I just don't understand it. I never used to get tired like this.

"Well, here comes some more Root Beer Scouts," she laughed, eyeing the group winding its way past the paddle fence toward the tent. "Have a nice trip back—and say hello to Laurel and Gladys if you see 'em."

"Sure will."

The Scout leader offered a cheery greeting as we passed the line of giggling kids. Dressed in various parts of Scout uniforms, St. Louis Cardinals baseball caps, mud-streaked sneakers, and blue neckerchiefs, they obviously were having a fabulous time.

The sun stood almost overhead, the day turning into a scorcher, as we pushed our canoe off and headed west. With lots of time, we swung past the dock, paused to look at the big island, the rickety bridges, then surveyed Dorothy's winter cabin, gray and weathered in the shade of the big pines. To the uneducated eye the grounds probably looked like a junkyard, but every item held a host of memories, and accompanying stories, for Dorothy. The first snow machine welded together by Chester Maser in 1954 lay half-covered by a tattered piece of canvas. Old sleds used to haul firewood lay upended, one with a single rusted runner pointing skyward, the other missing. Hanging from a tree was the frame of an aluminum landing net, the netting long gone; half of a fiberglass fishing rod rested against the trunk below. Clamped to a board between two trees was most of a nonoperable Evinrude outboard motor with the propeller and lower gear unit missing. But with all the assorted stuff, not a scrap of candy wrapper or cigarette stub lay anywhere on the ground. Dorothy always drew a very sharp line between her "junk" and litter.

For Lil and me, the paddle homeward took place mostly in silence. We paused at the Seed Lake Portage for sandwiches and lemonade. On the far shore, newly minted green rushes nodded in the breeze. A hen black duck led a single file of seven youngsters around the edge of a fallen jack pine. "Suppose Dorothy will come out this winter to stay?" Lil asked between bites of her sandwich.

"Don't know. She ought to; but then, she's pretty stubborn. Her whole life is up there on those islands. She's said a hundred times she can't seem to stand the city any more."

Again I thought of those once-powerful hands, hands that gripped a splitting ax like a seasoned lumberjack, hands that flipped up a ninety-pound canoe like a feather—the same hands that could gently splint a broken wing or stroke life back into a half-frozen bird. I thought of the faded *Saturday Evening Post* photo on the wall of the cabin, a photo of a fine-looking dark-haired young lady in her twenties, holding up a mammoth forty-pound lake trout.

The sun still sparkled on the water—like a million diamonds,

THE FINAL CHAPTER

Dorothy would say. The trees were green with spring's new growth, the air sweet and fresh, the clouds a few cotton balls bouncing across an endless blue sky. "It is like the Ojibwa say," I thought. "Only the sun and the earth last forever."

A week after we got back to Moose Lake, I checked in with Kawishiwi District Forest Ranger Roger Baker in Ely. "We visited Dorothy last week," I said. "She's showing signs of wear and tear."

Roger ran a hand through his thatch of straw-colored hair. "We were up there and talked with her but she wants to stay. We're flying in all the supplies she needs and we've got her fixed up with a radio to call out regularly. We're doing all we can to see she is comfortable."

Fall came. Lil and I never got back up to Isle of Pines. Forest Service crews began flying in supplies. The government's Beaver float plane took in 1,200 pounds of corn, 500 pounds of sunflower seeds, 350 pounds of sugar (for next summer's root beer), cases of toilet paper, cases of paper towels, radio batteries, shiny new pipe sections for the barrel stove, and six 100-pound cylinders of propane fuel. Forester Jim Hinds, who flew in with the loads, said Dorothy was bright and cheerful and looking forward to coming out for a Christmas visit to Chicago.

Winter came raging in the first of December 1986, freezing the lakes shut and piling snow high in the forest. Deer headed for their cedar swamp yarding areas. Ruffed grouse dove headfirst into snowdrifts at night to escape the bitter chill. Dorothy's bird feeder worked overtime, crowded with chickadees, nuthatches, grosbeaks, and redpolls. Dorothy's former Angels—the snowmobilers who had come up through the years when snowmobiles were allowed—occasionally met on the street and wondered, "How do you suppose Dorothy is doing?"

From up on Knife Lake, the radio called in its message to Kawishiwi Headquarters more or less regularly, and plans were being made to fly up and get Dorothy for her Christmas trip. But on Friday, December 14, no radio contact was made. This was not unusual. Sometimes Dorothy was too busy; sometimes she simply forgot to change the batteries. No one was on duty at the Kawishiwi office on Saturday and Sunday, but on Monday, December 17, there was still no contact. Now concerned, Jim Hinds and USFS pilot Doug Bowman rolled the Beaver out on the ice of Shagawa Lake, warmed up the engine, and took off for Knife Lake. It had turned unexpectedly overcast and rainy. As the plane droned over Hoist Bay of Basswood Lake, ice began forming on the wings. Bowman shook his head. "Can't make it," he noted grimly, radioed the base, and headed back to Ely.

During the night, the rain changed to snow and the weather turned colder. At dawn, Hinds and Bowman, accompanied by Jerry Jussila, took off from Shagawa Lake. The weather was better for flying, and the Beaver made good time cruising over a landscape newly decorated with a fresh layer of snow. At the east end of Knife Lake, Bowman dipped and banked over the island. A feeling of apprehension filled the plane. No smoke rose from the stovepipe on Dorothy's cabin. Worse yet, no tracks marked the fresh snow.

Knife Lake, always late to freeze, had just recently iced over, and Bowman didn't think the surface would support the plane. But nearby Portage Lake had frozen weeks earlier, and he brought the ship in over the treeline, dropping the skis smoothly onto the snow. The pilot cut the ignition, and the clatter of the big DeHaviland motor ceased as the prop slowed and stopped. Wordlessly, the three men climbed down, crossed the portage, and trudged toward Pine Island.

"It was the longest walk of my life," Hinds commented later. "It is only a half mile, but it seemed like we were walking through the snow forever."

The cabin was silent as they approached. A chickadee fluttered near the empty bird feeder by the kitchen window. The men glanced at each other, then strode up the wooden steps and onto the porch. Stamping snow off their boots, they hesitantly approached the door. Never locked, it opened with a light push. Inside, the enameled coffeepot sat on the cold stove. The tin wash basin hung on its customary nail. The kitchen table held its usual clutter—letters, magazines, and jars. In the middle sat the radio.

"Dorothy?" Jerry said softly as they stepped into the room. Then they saw the crumpled form on the floor. She was wearing her heavy jacket and had apparently come in from outside when that great heart simply gave out.

The men stood in a long, awkward silence before they radioed their sad report to headquarters. A deputy sheriff would be on the way up. The coroner would be notified. A phone call would go out to Dorothy's family, waiting in Chicago for her Christmas visit.

The chickadee in the empty bird feeder pecked impatiently at the window. But no more seeds would fill the feeder. Ever. The final curtain had descended on a half century of drama at Isle of Pines on Knife Lake.

THIS IS THE FORMER HOMESITE
OF DOROTHY MOLTER. YOU ARE
WELCOME TO PAY YOUR RESPECTS
BUT PLEASE NO CAMPING

Epilogue

Wᴵᴸᴰᴇʀɴᴇss ᴘᴀᴅᴅʟᴇʀs currently stopping at the Isle of Pines will find little to indicate that this was once the dwelling place of Knife Lake's famous "Root Beer Lady." Well back from the shoreline, the Forest Service has erected a modest sign, which reads: "THIS IS THE FORMER HOMESITE OF DOROTHY MOLTER. YOU ARE WELCOME TO PAY YOUR RESPECTS, BUT PLEASE, NO CAMPING."

The cabins were carefully dismantled during the winter of 1987 and hauled by dogsled and snowmobile over the ice to Moose Lake, and from there by truck to Ely, where they have been restored as a museum adjacent to the International Wolf Center. In the spring of 1992, the Dorothy Molter Memorial Fund, administered jointly by her family and friends and the Forest Service, helped supply thirty thousand pine seedlings for replanting in and adjacent to the Boundary Waters Canoe Area Wilderness. These pines will provide future nesting sites for the descendants of Baldy the Bald Eagle and will ensure, to some measure, that the spirit of Dorothy Molter lives on.